W9-AAH-751

California's
Arab Americans

a prequel to

California: An International Community
Understanding Our Diversity

Janice Marschner

CALIFORNIA'S ARAB AMERICANS. Copyright © 2003 by Coleman Ranch Press. All rights reserved. Printed in the United States of America. No part of this book may be used or reproduced in any manner without written permission except for brief quotations used in critical articles and reviews. For information:

Coleman Ranch Press, P. O. Box 1496, Sacramento, CA 95812
1.877.7OLDCAL or colemanranch@comcast.net

Coleman Ranch Press books may be purchased for educational, business, or sales promotional use. For information please write: Special Markets Department, Coleman Ranch Press, P. O. Box 1496, Sacramento, CA 95812.

FIRST EDITION

Cover Design by Robert L. Goodman, Silvercat

Cover photograph:
  Davis Schemoon Family in Eureka, courtesy of Jerry Colivas

Library of Congress Cataloging-in-Publication Data

Marschner, Janice
  California's Arab Americans / Janice Marschner. — 1st ed.

  ISBN 0-9677069-7-1

Library of Congress Control Number: 2003095123

Website: www.CRPRESS.com

"Be proud of being an American,
but also be proud that
your fathers and mothers
came from a land upon which
God laid His precious hand
and raised His messengers."

Excerpt from Kahlil Gibran's poem,
I Believe in You, written for the first
edition of *Syrian World Magazine*
published in Brooklyn, NY in 1926

Contents

Preface

ORIGINALLY MY next book was going to reveal the allure of the early hot springs resorts in California. While researching my first book, *California 1850 – A Snapshot in Time*, I kept running across mention of these glorious resorts.

About 75 of these resorts opened in the late 1800s/ early 1900s and 25 of them remain in operation today. This will be a fun and interesting project. Stay tuned.

However, after the tragedy of September 11, 2001, I suspended my hot springs research and began work on another book I had contemplated four years ago. I had been noticing that there were areas of California that had concentrations of particular ethnic groups—Sikhs in Yuba City, Hmong in the Central Valley, Armenians in Los Angeles and Fresno, and many of almost every ethnic group in my hometown, Sacramento.[1] I wondered why and when the various groups arrived. Why did they settle in certain areas?[2]

Following 9/11 there was a reported rise in hate crimes against Middle Eastern Americans—Arabs, Afghans, Sikhs, South Asians, and also others mistaken for Arabs or Muslims. I recalled my earlier idea for a book about California's immigrants, and decided it should be written now, not later. Perhaps there are others like me who have not picked up a

1 In 2002 *Time* magazine reported that The Civil Rights Project at Harvard University identified Sacramento as the most ethnically and culturally diverse city in the most ethnically and culturally diverse state in the nation.
2 California recently became the first state in the union to have no majority racial/ ethnic group.

sociology textbook since California became so diverse; maybe others have similar questions.

The book, in progress, *California: An International Community, Understanding Our Diversity*, will help all Americans understand how America became one of the most diverse nations in the world. The explanation is found in the various changes made to U.S. immigration law since 1819, the particular labor needs of America during different times in history, economic incentives made available to immigrants, humanitarian outreach made to refugees from different parts of the world, as well as other historic events.

The introduction of *California: An International Community* will summarize the historical roots of our diversity and the other chapters will provide details about each ethnic group.

Well into that book project, while researching California's Arab Americans, I discovered that little had ever been written about this ethnic group. Only recently have school text-books and American history books included any significant information about them—thus my decision to write this separate book—*California's Arab Americans*.

The Arab-American community itself has traditionally downplayed its heritage—choosing instead to assimilate and integrate into American society, refraining from recognition of its presence and contributions. This changed after 9/11 when prejudice against Arab Americans increased. Hate crimes were ignited by the tragic events, but were already anchored by negative and inaccurate pre-conceptions about Muslims and Arabs—even Christian Arabs.

After 9/11, Arab and particularly Muslim organizations reached out to schools, churches, clubs, and other community organizations in an attempt to educate and build relationships with society at large.

When discussing my Arab-American project with people, I heard complaints that Arab Americans failed to "explain themselves" after 9/11. From my research, especially on the Internet, I know now that such outreach was attempted, but the efforts did not connect with the general public.

I hope that this book, some of which will be excerpted in *California: An International Community,* will provide Californians and all Americans with a better understanding about our community members of Arab descent—the now third and fourth generation, as well as new arrivals. It is evident that Arab Americans have been making positive contributions to our state and country ever since they began arriving in the late 19th century.

Researching Arab Americans, and especially California's Arab Americans, was a challenging task. The two main resources I used to learn about the early arrival of Arabs in America were the works of Adele L. Younis and Alixa Neff. Philip M. Kayal, of the Center for Migration Studies in New York, designated the late Younis as the dean of early Arab-American studies. Neff, a Lebanese American herself, continues to be among the most noted historians specializing in Arab-American culture.

David Lamb's *The Arabs — Journeys Beyond the Mirage* provided an excellent overview of the contemporary Middle East. I also skimmed a number of juvenile cultural history series books for a glimpse at the history and society of the various contemporary Arab countries. One children's book that leaves you with a very positive impression about Arab Americans in general is Brent Ashabranner's *An Ancient Heritage: The Arab-American Minority.* (It is good to know that these types of books are available to our young people.)

Gregory Orfalea's *Before the Flames: A Quest for the History of Arab-Americans* was one of the few books with any substantial information specific to Arabs in California.

A considerable amount has been written about Arab Americans on the east coast and in the mid-west, particularly the Detroit area, which until recently, had the highest concentration of Arab Americans. (Los Angeles now has the largest Arab population in the United States.)

Several internet sites provided information about successful contemporary Arab-American Californians. Arab internet sites were valuable resources about current issues and mores relating to the Arab world and Arab Americans.

Arab-American almanacs and encyclopedias such as the periodic *Arab American Almanac* published by The News Circle Publishing House and the *Arab American Encyclopedia* published by the Arab Community Center for Economic and Social Services, as well as the various Gale Group publications on Arab Americans, were also quite informative. The News Circle Publishing House will be releasing the Fifth Edition of its almanac in 2003.

Finally, the 1939-40 and 1948-1950 directories compiled by Archpriest Elias Sady of Saint George's Church in Los Angeles helped me focus on particular city and county histories. These two publications, available for viewing at the California State Library in Sacramento, list the American Arabic-speaking people from Syria, Lebanon, Palestine, and Jordan living and doing business in California in those years.

I scoured local history books, library collections, and the internet for references to the family names listed in these directories. I also inquired of local historical societies for information about these families, and personally contacted over 300 families by mail, e-mail, or telephone. I am grateful to those who responded. I collected accounts about a cross-section of Arab-American families throughout the state.

This book condenses a substantial amount of historical information about the complex Arab world. I do not mean to imply that the subject matter is simple; it is not. There are many more paths I could have explored. There is much more all of us can discover about the places of origin of this ethnic group. Media coverage during the 2003 war in Iraq probably helped many in that regard.

If this book dispels some of the misconceptions and prejudices associated with our fellow Americans of Arab descent, my time in research and writing will have been well spent. Hopefully Arab Americans will gain some new knowledge about their ethnic heritage in the United States and about the earliest settlers in California whose claimed homeland was a region of the Arab world.

Acknowledgments are always difficult for authors to make when their works are finally completed, because they are exhausted and anxious to get the book to the printer. They fear that in their haste, they may leave someone out. That is my fear as I write this, but here is my best effort.

I have already mentioned some of the publications that were helpful; the bibliography lists all of the resources used. A few local historical societies were extremely helpful, including the Humboldt County Historical Society, the Martinez Historical Society, the Plumas County Museum, the San Diego Historical Society, the Shasta Historical Society, the Vista Historical Society, and Simone Wilson of the Sonoma County Historical Journal. Genealogy e-mail group members contributed some useful insights, as well—Vernon Brown, Ronald Morgan, Dennis Freeman, and Harleigh Winkler.

I am grateful to all of the Arab Americans who shared their family histories and photographs with me— Lori Abdelnour, Nicholas Ayoob, Phil and Doris Bracken, Jerry Colivas, Meg and Tom Farrage, Joseph Farrah, Peter Fatooh, Joe Ganim, Marilyn Habeeb, Elias W. "Chuck" Haddad, George, Adele, and George M. Bud Homsy; Joan and Bill Kassis, Winnie Kingsbury, Barbara

Lithin, Gail Malouf, Kais Menoufy, Dorothy McDonald, Barbara Moses, Jane and Jim Naify, Theodore D. Nasser, Alma Rashid, James and Audrey Romley, Dona Shaieb, Kamel Shelhoup, Willard F. Zahn, M.D.; and Virginia Zlaket.

The comments from several of them painted a positive and optimistic picture: "We love our culture, our traditions. We are proud of our family and what we accomplished." From another long time family: "These were proud people. There was no welfare system and they did not want welfare. They wanted to work—become educated—and become citizens in this great country." A fairly new arrival wrote: "California is a great state with lots of opportunities."

Professor Ayad Al-Qazzaz, Dr. and Ms. Metwalli B. Amer, and Joseph R. Haiek—thank you for your tremendous encouragement and sharing of resources.

Finally, once again my entire family endured through another project that took time away that I might otherwise have spent with them. My son, Jason, who has visited the Middle East recently and often, courtesy of the U.S. Air Force Reserve, often allowed, "Well, I'll let you get back to your writing." (My daughter, Julie, living out-of-town, was busy herself training for marathons and conducting genetic research.) My mother, Marie Nelson, encouraged me to keep seeking the personal histories because she especially enjoys reading biographies. And my dear husband, Jeff, besides encouraging me through this project, applied his usual excellent editing skills. Thank you one and all.

Janice Marschner
Sacramento, California
September 2003

Introduction

THE INDIVIDUAL FAMILY histories representing a cross-section of Arab American families throughout the state make this book unique. Before reading these stories, it would be helpful for the reader to become familiar with geographical, sociological, and historical facts about the Arab world. A concise summary of this information is set forth in chapters 1 through 4.

Chapter 5 outlines where the major populations of Arab Americans live in California today.

Chapters 6 through 15 contain the individual family histories. The chapters correspond to the customary regional divisions of the state, starting on the north coast.

Sidebars placed throughout the book provide more detailed information about topics such as Arabic writing and names; clarification about who the Syrians, Palestinians, and Arab Afghans are; the basic tenets of Islam and Islamic fundamentalism; Arab American organizations; well-known Arab Americans; and the characteristics of Arab cuisine, dress, and family structure. One sidebar discusses the early and current involvement of Arab Americans in the film industry, especially in the ownership of theater chains.

An extensive bibliography will assist those wishing to do further research on this long-neglected topic.

Finally, an index references every surname mentioned in the book, and every place of origin, both in the Arab world and in North America, if such is noted for a particular family. Every California city and town mentioned is listed, as well as a few topics of particular interest.

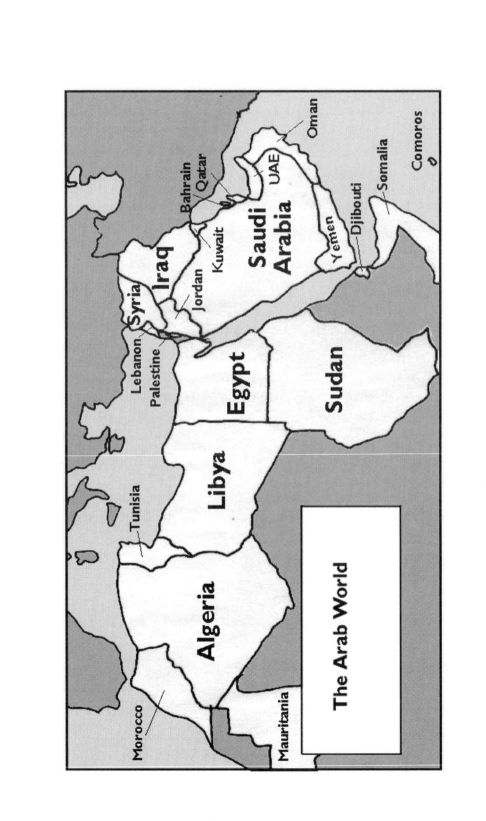

The Arab World

Morocco
Mauritania
Algeria
Tunisia
Libya
Egypt
Sudan
Palestine
Lebanon
Syria
Iraq
Jordan
Kuwait
Bahrain
Qatar
Saudi Arabia
UAE
Oman
Yemen
Djibouti
Somalia
Comoros

CHAPTER ONE

Countries of Origin of Arab Americans

A FUNDAMENTAL misconception many have about Arab Americans is where they or their ancestors came from. Today, most Arab Americans were born in the United States—perhaps 63 percent of the estimated two to three million Americans who trace their roots to one of the current 21 Arab countries[3] in North and East Africa, southwestern Asia, and the Arabian Peninsula.

People with origins in one of the Arab countries identify with that country (claim it as their nationality), but also consider themselves as Arabs generally. With the rise of Islam in the seventh century A.D. throughout Africa and Asia (as well as Europe), the conquered peoples of the Middle East and Africa adopted the Arabic language and many of the characteristics of the Arab culture.

The countries on the African continent that are part of the modern Arab world are Mauritania, Morocco, Algeria, Tunisia, Libya,[4] Egypt, Sudan, Djibouti, Somalia, and Comoros. Those located in southwestern Asian are Jordan, Lebanon, Syria, Iraq, Kuwait, Saudi Arabia, United Arab Emirates, Qatar, and Bahrain. The Arabian Peninsula contains the Arab countries of Yemen and Oman. The Arab world also includes the territories known as the Gaza Strip and the West Bank (formerly Judea and Samaria), where Palestinians seek to establish an independent state of their own on the site of Bethlehem and the Old City of Jerusalem.

---

[3] There are 22 Arab countries if Palestine is counted as a country. See page 9.
[4] The "Arab West" region of North Africa, composed of Mauritania, Morocco, Algeria, Tunisia, and Libya, is called the Maghrib.

4

The Arab world is also home to non-Arab ethnic groups like the Chaldeans,[5] Assyrians,[6] Kurds,[7] Berbers,[8] and Armenians.[9] Some of the Arab world area is also known as the "Middle East"[10] or West Asia, but the Middle East also includes the non-Arab countries of Israel, Cyprus, Turkey,[11] Armenia, Azerbaijan, Iran,[12] Turkmenistan, Uzbekistan, Kyrgyzstan, Tajikistan, Afghanistan, and Pakistan.[13]

The largest number of Arab Americans trace their roots to Lebanon,[14] but many others come from Syria, Egypt, Jordan, Iraq, Yemen, and the area known as Palestine. Smaller numbers come from other Arab countries.

[5] Chaldeans are Christians from northern Iraq. The native language is Chaldean, but they also must learn Arabic in school. In Iraq, Chaldeans are religiously distinct from the Muslim majority. However, Chaldeans do have an Iraqi nationality and some shared interests with Arabs. When Chaldeans emigrate to America they usually are classified as Arab or Iraqi, but they really do not consider themselves to be Arab. They will be described in a separate chapter in the forthcoming book, *California: An International Community*.

[6] Assyrians live in northern Syria, northern Iraq, Turkey, and Iran. They speak Assyrian, an Aramaic subgroup similar to Chaldean. They do not consider themselves Arabs and will be described along with the Chaldeans in the forthcoming book.

[7] Kurds live in northern Syria, northern Iraq, Turkey, Iran, and Armenia. They speak Indo-European languages, but also learn Arabic in school.

[8] Berbers live in the Maghrib region of North Africa and speak Berber, a branch of the Afro-Asiatic linguistic family, as well as Arabic.

[9] Armenians from Lebanon, Syria, Egypt, Jordan, Iraq, and Palestine are Christians whose families arrived in 1918 as survivors of the massacres in Turkey. They speak Armenian, and also Arabic.

[10] The Middle East, as well as the Near East and the Far East, are British colonial concepts that refer to parts of the world "east" of England.

[11] Turkey also is considered part of Central Asia and Europe.

[12] Contrary to popular belief, Iran is not an Arab country. It was formed out of the Persian Empire and its dominant language is Farsi, not Arabic. Similarly, Afghans, Sikhs, and other South Asians are not Arabs.

[13] There is disagreement about which countries make up the modern definition of the Middle East. Some include Egypt and other northern African countries; some do not; and some consider Armenia and Azerbaijan to be part of Europe.

[14] Early Arab immigrants from Lebanon were from a part of geographic Syria known as Mount Lebanon, which became part of the separate state of Lebanon after World War I.

Although Arabs are distinguishable from one another racially, ethnically, religiously, historically, and politically, they share a common culture and language—Arabic, and consider themselves to be one nationality. It was not until the early part of the 20th century that Arabic-speaking people were identified as Arab rather than members of a family, village, or religious sect. However, it still is difficult to group all Arabs into one community since there are so many differences among them.

Arabs may have white skin and blue eyes, or olive or dark skin and brown eyes. Hair textures vary. They may be of black African stock or Asian with Chinese features. The United States has, at different times, classified Arab immigrants as African, Asian, white, European or as belonging to a separate group. (See pages 31-32.)

Derivatives of the Word "Arab" and their Meaning

- Arab is a noun for a person and when referring to an Arab American, hyphenation is not necessary. (When ethnicity or nationality are relevant, the country should be specified by using Lebanese, Syrian, Jordanian, Yemeni, etc.)
- Arab may be used as an adjective, as in "Arab country," and when used as an adjective in conjunction with American, Arab-American often is hyphenated, as in Arab-American concerns, but not always.
- Arabic is the name of the language and generally is not used as an adjective.
- Arabian is an adjective that refers to Saudi Arabia, the Arabian Peninsula, or as in Arabian horse.

Consequently, most early Arab immigrants are referred to as Syrians, but the Lebanese, as they are known today, actually were the earliest to arrive. (Lebanon has also been the most impacted by the Arab-Israeli conflict and by its own internal conflicts arising from religious differences—all of which have prompted the migration of many Lebanese.)

Arabic Writing and Names

- Arabic is one of several languages written from right to left.
- Arabic is written in the 28-character Arabic alphabet; English is written in Latin characters.
- Arabic letters are connected like script. Fine writing is called calligraphy and is held in high regard and appreciated as an art form in the Arab culture, especially since the Qur'an forbids making pictures or statues of living things to discourage the worship of idols. Arab artists instead create artistic designs using the beautiful Arabic letters—carving words in stone for decoration or weaving verses into rugs.

In the Name of Allah, the
Most Merciful, and the
Forever Merciful.
Praise Be to Allah, Lord of
the worlds.

لا إله إلا الله محمد رسول الله

There is no deity except Allah; and Muhammad
is the Messenger of Allah.

Pilgrimage thereto is a
duty men owe to
Allah, those who can
afford the journey.

- Because Arabic and English characters and sounds are different, there is more than one way to transliterate the words. The Associated Press, for example, recently changed its style for the spelling of Mohammed to Muhammad, Moslem to Muslim, and Koran to Qur'an.

(Continued)

Arabic Writing and Names (Continued)

- Many Arab immigrants retained their Arabic names, but the spellings of the same name often differed and often depended on how an immigration official interpreted what he heard the immigrant say. The name Khouri, for example, can be spelled as Khoury, Khuri, Couri, Koory, or Corey. (Harik 46) Other variations of common names in California are Abood and Aboud; Ayoob and Ayoub; Ghanem, Ganim, and Gannam; Maloof, Malouf, and Mallouf; Nassar, Nasser, and Nassour; Schemoon and Shamoon; and Zien and Zine.
- Many people changed their names to the English equivalent in meaning or sound. The common name Haddad became "Smith," and Ashshi became "Cook." The English names of Sawyer, Thomas, Joseph, George, and Abbott were formerly Sawaya, Tuma, Yusuf, Jirjus, and Abboud, respectively.
- Today Arabs seldom "Americanize" their names. Personal names include paternal genealogy and may also indicate family name, tribal affiliation, and village or region of origin.
- For example, a man named Abd al Rahman bin (or ben) Qasim bin Muhammad El (or Al) Bayadh is the son of Qasim, the grandson of Muhammad, and a native of the town of El Bayadh. (The word bin means "son of.") The man would be addressed as Mister Abd al Rahman.
- In spoken Arabic, names are slurred. For example, Abd al Rahman is pronounced "Abdur Rahman."
- Westerners assume incorrectly that Abdal (or Abdul) is the first name and that Rahman is his last name.
- Many Arabic names, such as the one in this example, are designations of the attributes of God (Allah). Abd al means "servant of" and Rahman means "merciful"; thus the name literally means "the servant of the Merciful (God)." (Kagda 93)
- Sometimes the birth of the first son means so much to the family that the parents may become known by the child's name. For example, if a man Hisham names his first son Saad, the man could become known as Abu Saad, "father of Saad"; Saad's mother would then be known as Umm Saad, "Mother of Saad." (Fox 82)

Who Are Arab Afghans?

- Since 9/11 there has been confusion about the people of Afghanistan since that is where the al-Qaeda and Osama Bin Laden were operating.
- Afghans themselves are not Arabs. The Pashtun people, generally Sunni Muslims, form the dominant ethnic and linguistic community located in Southern Asia.
- The term "Arab Afghan" refers to Arab men who went to Afghanistan to participate in the war against the Soviets. Volunteers—many of them teenagers—traveled to Afghanistan throughout the late 1970s and '80s with help from the United States, Pakistan, Saudi Arabia, Egypt, and Kuwait. All of these countries were supplying and training anti-Communist Mujahideen (or Mujahidin) forces.
- After helping the Afghans defeat the Russian-allied government, most Afghan Arabs returned home, but some remained in Afghanistan.
- After the Soviet withdrawal from Afghanistan in 1989, foreign aid to the Mujahideen decreased and then was eliminated almost entirely due to various issues arising during the Gulf War.
- Fighting continued among the various Mujahideen factions, and when the fundamentalist Islamic Taliban movement captured Kabul in 1996 from the Mujahideen, many Afghan Arabs joined the Taliban.
- Throughout the 1980s, the Afghan Arabs had called themselves by the Arabic term Anssar, meaning "supporters," which referred to support for Afghans against the Soviets. Bin Laden's organization used the name until 1990, when it was changed to al-Qaeda, which means "the base." The change signified a dramatic shift in objectives and marked the point when the organization first became hostile towards the United States. Arab Afghans were expanding support for Islamic fundamentalists worldwide. Jihad ("holy war")[15] operations began to be planned and organized against the perceived enemies of Muslims around the globe.

---

[15] Most Muslims interpret *jihad* as the "struggle" or "exerted effort" to follow their faith, live in a manner consistent with the Qur'an, and struggle to improve the quality of life in society. The Qur'an does not advocate "holy war," but self-defense is justified if one is attacked or oppressed by an unjust regime. Jihad also is not a war to force the Muslim faith on others.

(Continued opposite.)

Who Are Palestinians?

- Palestine has never been a sovereign state and Palestinians are not a separate race. A Palestinian was originally a citizen (Jew, Christian, or Arab) of a distinct region under the Ottoman Turkish Empire, which later became the British-mandated territory of Palestine (1922-48).
- In 1948 when the Jewish state of Israel was created, many Arab Palestinians were displaced to various Arab countries and lost official recognition of their nationality; now when they immigrate they are listed as citizens of those various Arab countries. (Many Palestinians chose to remain in Israel, however, and became citizens of the new country.)
- Generally a Palestinian is a Muslim or Christian native or descendant of a native of the area within Israel, East Jerusalem, the West Bank, and the Gaza Strip and the part of Jordan west of the Jordan River. (In the Bible, it is the area referred to as Canaan.) Christian and Muslim immigrants from Israel are much more likely to identify themselves as Palestinian or to use some label other than Israeli, because the latter term connotes the Jewish dominance of Israel. Technically, though, some Arabs are Israeli citizens.
- Today the Palestinian National Authority acts as the government for a people seeking independence and self-rule. The progress made in 2003 of realizing this goal surpasses that of any other time in history.

Who Are Arab Afghans? (Continued)

- After the Gulf War in 1991, Americans became the primary enemy of the Arab Afghans for three main reasons: U.S. military presence in Saudi Arabia; America's unconditional support of Israel; and the ongoing sanctions against Iraq.
- Following 9/11, the U.S. presence in Afghanistan exacerbated the situation. Taliban and al-Qaeda infrastructures in Afghanistan were destroyed, but most of the Afghan Arab fighters fled to other parts of the world. Now al-Qaeda possesses a network of trained and experienced members who can be mobilized to execute operations globally.

Adapted with permission from
"'Arab Afghan' Primer—Who Are the Ones Who Got Away?"
by Jalal Ghazi, Pacific News Service (PNS), 29 March 2002

CHAPTER TWO

Religions of Arab Americans

TODAY MORE than 90% of the population of the Arab world is Muslim. The two other monotheistic religions—Judaism and Christianity—also had their origins in this part of the world. Thus, some Arabs are Christians of various sects, especially in Lebanon, Syria, Iraq, Palestine, and Jordan; others are Jewish.

St. Nicholas Antiochian Orthodox Church in San Francisco. Established in 1930, it is the most prominent Arab-American Christian church in the San Francisco Bay Area.

Originally, the majority of Arab Americans were Christian of the Eastern-rite sects—Maronite, Catholic Orthodox (Melkites), Syrian Orthodox (Jacobites), Antiochian Orthodox, and Apostolic Armenians, who had migrated to Syria in 1918 as survivors of the massacres in Turkey. Others were Chaldean, Roman, Armenian, Arab, and Syrian

11

Catholics; Coptic, Greek and Assyrian Orthodox; or Anglican (English Protestant).

Christian Arabs often attended American churches, but whenever a sizable number of Arabs settled in a community, churches of their respective faiths were established. Most of the Eastern-rite sects eventually Americanized their rites—even translating their liturgy into English.[16]

Early Muslim Arab immigrants had no place to worship until mosques were created.[17] The first mosque in America was established in Highland Park, Michigan, in 1919. Today there are mosques (*masjids*) and Islamic centers in major cities across the country, including over 100 in California alone.

Mosques can be small, prefab buildings, grand monumental structures, or anything in between, including former fire stations, theaters, warehouses, and shops. Most of

the classical architectural structures were built after 1965, which coincided with the general interest in and acceptance of differing

King Fahd Mosque in Culver City, Los Angeles County, built in 1998.
(Photograph courtesy of You Jae Ryuk/TheimageAsia.com)

[16] Christian Arab Americans of the Eastern-rite sects observe the major Christian holidays. However, the Eastern-rite churches celebrate Christmas on the Epiphany, January 6th, and they use a different moon definition to determine the date of Easter.
[17] For many years, most Muslim immigrants tried to conceal their religious and ethnic identities by changing their names to make them sound more American and by refraining from participating in religious practices or wearing traditional clothing that would make them appear "different" from the average citizen.

ethnicities and religions in America. Muslims were finally able to focus on ministering to their community and maintaining their traditions, discarding prior concerns about being different. In addition to mosques, Muslim community centers and schools were established and Arabic language classes offered.

Today in most communities, there are more Muslim Arab Americans than Christian Arab Americans. The Muslim Arab Americans share their faith with many other American ethnic groups, as well— Indonesians, Malaysians, Indo-Pakistanis, Iranians, other East Asians, eastern Europeans, and sub-Saharan Africans.[18]

SALAM Community Center in Sacramento. SALAM stands for Sacramento Area League of Associated Muslims; it was founded by Dr. Metwalli B. Amer in 1987.

[18] Most African American Muslims in the United States are not part of the Nation of Islam, which is a separate African American religious group begun in the 20th century with some different practices than those followed by other Muslims. A large number of African American members of the Nation of Islam, led by W. Deen Muhammad, converted to orthodox Sunni Islam in 1975, upon the death of Muhammad's father, Elijah Muhammad, the founder of the Nation of Islam.

Islam

- Islam is a major world religion, second only to Christianity in number, with more than a billion adherents. Most of the Islamic population is African or Asian, including Persians, Turks, Malaysians, Indo-Pakistanis, Indonesians, and Chinese. The remainder of Muslims are spread throughout the former Soviet Union, Europe, and North America. Only about 20% of Muslims are Arab. (Gerner 2)

- Unlike most other religions, Islam does not have a top leader. Muslim mosques and associations are independent of one another. Furthermore, Muslims are not required to be members of a mosque.

- An *imam* is the leader of prayer at a mosque and he delivers a sermon (*khutbah*) on Fridays, the holiest day of the Islamic week. In many American mosques, the *imam* also serves as the mosque's administrator.

- In the United States, Islamic centers usually serve all Muslim groups, but some may be broken down by country of origin and period of immigration. Smaller groups of immigrants from such countries as Morocco, Yemen, Algiers, and Iraq establish their own mosques, which may also vary by sect—Sunni, Shi'ite, or Druze.

- Like Christianity, there are divisions within Islam. Sunnis and Shi'ites have differing opinions or beliefs about a number of political and theological issues, including the line of succession of the prophet Muhammad.[19] Most Muslims worldwide and in the United States are Sunni, but Sunni and Shi'ites worship together in the same mosques.

- The Druze, with one million adherents worldwide, is an independent branch of Islam that incorporates elements of other Eastern religions. One can only become a Druze by birth, not conversion, so beliefs have historically been kept secret. However, American Druze have come to realize that some explanation of their faith improves their public image. Southern California is home to the largest Druze population in the United States; the first Druze Cultural Center opened in Eagle Rock, California in 1993.

- Islam follows a lunar calendar and its year contains 11 fewer days than the Gregorian calendar. The first day of the year one is the day

[19] Muhammad was a prophet of Islam; he is not regarded as a deity to be worshipped. Members of the Islamic faith are correctly called Muslims, not Moslems or Mohammedans. (Continued)

Islam (Continued)

Muhammad left Mecca for Medina. (By the Gregorian calendar this was on July 16, 622 A.D.) Called the *Hegira*, which is Arabic for "migration," it was the day he fled Mecca to avoid a plot to kill him because Meccans believed he was either lying about the divine revelations he received from Allah, or that he was deranged. However, Muhammad was enthusiastically received in Medina and became the city's ruler.

- In 630 A.D., after spreading his teachings throughout the Middle East and most of North Africa, Muhammad returned to Mecca. Islam had a profound cultural and political impact on the Middle East, at last providing a common heritage to the diverse region.

- Muhammad, who was illiterate, had a scribe write down the revelations that he received from Allah through the Angel Gabriel, which constitute the Qur'an (also spelled Koran). For Muslims the Qur'an is the final word of God, replacing and correcting the Old and New Testaments of the Bible and any other holy books. Arabic is Islam's sacred language and any version of the Qur'an in another language is considered an interpretation of the Arabic words, not an exact translation. During the 1980s and '90s, however, American mosques and Islamic organizations increasingly began using English in their daily activities.

- *Islam* means "peace and submission to the will of God." Allah is the same as the God of Christians and Jews, and many prophets, traditions, and basic principles of justice, compassion, love, and honesty are shared with Christianity and Judaism. But the Qur'an is much more detailed about the rules and guidelines for daily life than the Christian Bible or Jewish Torah. This is because Islam is a way of life.

- There are five pillars of Islam—sacred obligations followers are expected to observe:

  1. *Shahada* - Profession of faith—there is no God but Allah, and Muhammad is his prophet.

  2. *Salah* - Praying five times a day in the correct manner.[20]

[20] In America, some dispensations have been known to be made for unusual circumstances and environments Muslims find themselves in—finding it difficult to bow in prayer five times a day, attending a mosque on Friday for community prayers (*jumaa*), etc. (Naff *Becoming American* 300).

Islam (Continued)

3. *Zakah* - Giving alms to the needy or to good causes.[21]

4. *Saum* – Observing the month of Ramadan[22] when God revealed the Qur'an to Muhammad over a 23-year period of time. This is the most important Muslim observance each year, and requires abstinence from food, drink, and sex between dawn and sunset for 29 or 30 days, pending moon phases. Feasts take place at night, however.

5. *Hajj* - Making the pilgrimage to Mecca (Makkah) in Saudi Arabia at least once in a lifetime—if one is physically and financially able to.

- Islamic law (*Shari'ah*) forbids adultery, gambling, usury (charging interest (*reba)* for loans,[23]) and the consumption of certain foods and alcohol.[24]

- Some Arab Muslim families celebrate the birth of Jesus at Christmas because they consider him to be an important prophet, as also mentioned in the Qur'an.

[21]*Zakah* is similar to the tithing of the Old Testament of the Bible. For Muslims, however, it usually is 2.5 percent of one's entire net wealth above and beyond one's needs, rather than ten percent of one's income. *Zakah* may be used to build mosques or other Islamic institutions, especially in non-Muslim countries. However, it is basically for people in need, especially Muslims. Some *zakah* may have inadvertently ended up in the hands of 9/11 hijackers, thus the cause for recent concern about the charitable intentions of certain Arab countries.

[22]Ramadan is the ninth month of the Islam calendar, and consequently falls at a different time of year according to the Gregorian calendar. It starts with the first sighting of the moon and ends at the sighting of the new moon. At this time the feast of *Eid al Fitr* (Feast of Breaking the Fast) is celebrated.

[23]Arabs finance business projects through installment sale, leasing, and/or equity participation. Islamic banks and their depositors share the financial risk and benefit with the entrepreneurs. Efforts are underway in the United States to devise alternative financing methods consistent with Islamic beliefs. An example of this is the American Finance House in Pasadena, California.

[24]The fact that Islam forbids the consumption of alcohol and that several Arab countries even outlaw it presents a spiritual and moral dilemma for many Arab Americans who make their living as grocery or liquor store owners.

Islamic Fundamentalism

- The growth of Islamic fundamentalism has posed a threat to the security of citizens living in the Middle East for several decades and has been a partial cause of Arab emigration from that region. (Since September 11, 2001, the entire world has viewed Islamic extremist groups as a threat to security.)

- Islamic fundamentalism is based on a literal interpretation of the Qur'an and the tradition of the Prophet Muhammad. The fundamentalists seek to halt economic and cultural progress and return to a state governed solely by strict Islamic law—*Shar'iah*. They see all western influence as sinful and decadent and want Islamic law to control the arts, education, culture, and lifestyles. Those who follow a less strict form of Islam have been pressured to change their behavior under threat of death. Intellectuals have been the most directly affected by Islamicist pressure.

- Islamic fundamentalists have formed over 30 extremist groups. The most widely known is al-Qaeda—the group established by Osama bin Ladin in the late 1980s to organize the Arab Mujahideen who fought in Afghanistan against the Soviet Union. Its current goal is to establish a pan-Islamic Caliphate[25] throughout the world by working with allied Islamic extremist groups to overthrow regimes it deems "non-Islamic" and expelling Westerners and non-Muslims from Muslim countries, including Saudi Arabia, Kuwait, Bahrain, and Oman, where U.S. military bases are located, as well as in Kashmir, Chechnya, and Israel.

- Above all, Islamic fundamentalists seek to destroy the United States, perceived as the source of immorality and anti-Muslim policies throughout the world. The extremists believe that it is the duty of all Muslims to kill U.S. citizens—civilian or military—and their allies everywhere.

- Al-Qaeda suicide attackers hijacked and crashed the four U.S. commercial jets on September 11th, directed the October 12, 2000 attack on the USS Cole in the port of Aden, Yemen; and conducted the bombings

[25] A pan-Islamic Caliphate would be an Islamic brotherhood and solidarity of a community of Muslims ruled by a secular and religious head of Islam.

(Continued)

Islamic Fundamentalism (Continued)

in August 1998 of the U.S. embassies in Nairobi, Kenya, and Dar es Salaam, Tanzania. It also claims to have shot down U.S. helicopters and killed U.S. servicemen in Somalia in 1993 and to have conducted three bombings that targeted U.S. troops in Aden, Yemen, in December 1992 ("Patterns of Global Terrorism Apr. 2002" website).

- A close partner of al-Qaeda is the Egyptian al-Jihad and Jama'ah al-Islamiyah [or al-Jihad] (the Islamic Group). The latter considers Sheik Omar Abdel Rahman to be its spiritual leader. He is currently serving a life sentence in a U.S. federal prison in connection with the 1993 bombing of the World Trade Center in New York City. Rahman, like bin Laden, justifies *jihad* against the West by calling it defensive, but he also claims that defensive actions are justified whenever people are attacked. In the opinion of Islamic fundamentalists, the West has "attacked" Islam. Unlike traditional Islam, they regard both Christians and Jews as enemies. The terrorists are opposed to the existence of Israel and any country friendly with Israel.

- There is also Hamas, which is a radical Islamic organization operating primarily in the Gaza Strip but also in the West Bank. It has played a major role in the violent terrorist operations against both Israelis and Arabs. Its highest priority is *jihad* for the liberation of Palestine and the establishment of an Islamic Palestine "from the Mediterranean Sea to the Jordan River." As a result of its subversive and terrorist activity, Hamas was outlawed in September 1989. Since the Gulf War, Hamas has been the leading perpetrator of terrorist activity in the area and is the strongest opposition group to the peace process. (*Hamas* means "courage and bravery" and is the Arabic acronym for "The Islamic Resistance Movement" (Harakat al-Muqawamah al-Islamiyya)) ("Hamas" International Policy Institute website).

- There also is an extremist Muslim Wahabi sect found primarily in Saudi Arabia. (Wahabism is Saudi Arabia's state religion and is taught in the schools.) Wahabi vigilantes identify themselves as *muwahiddun*.

CHAPTER THREE

Brief History of the Arab World

THE HISTORY of the Arab world dates back to the
Phoenicians in the 13th century B.C. and includes rule under
Assyria, Babylonia, the Persian Empire, and Alexander the
Great, thousands of years before Christ, as well as the Muslim
conquest of the seventh century A.D. This part of the world
also lived through the Crusades of the 11th through 13th
centuries, the Ottoman Empire of the 16th through early
20th centuries, and British, French, and Italian colonial rule
during the 19th and early 20th centuries.

Throughout this period of time, Arabs were contributing
to the progress of society by developing one of the first
written languages in history (Sumerian), creating algebra and
Arabic numerals, founding the first civilizations on earth—
Mesopotamia and Egypt; designing architecture that remains
renowned today—to name just a few of their accomplishments.

The Arab world has been especially important to the
rest of the world since the discovery of oil there in the
1920s and '30s. Today it is the center of the world's attention
because of the rise in world terrorism,[26] the 2003 war in
Iraq and the aftermath, and the continual turmoil stemming
from the Arab-Israeli conflict that has been raging for
over half a century.

The following timeline details some of the more significant events in the 20th century that led to the current turmoil
and that have prompted many of the more recent Arab

---

[26] Terrorists are of many different ethnicities and religions, however, and operate all
over the world, not just from the Arab world or just from the Middle East.

immigrants to abandon their homelands for America and other parts of the world.

Historical Timeline

1917 Balfour Declaration – Britain supports Jewish homeland in Palestine; European Jews begin moving into Palestine

1947 United Nations votes to partition Palestine into Arab and Jewish states

1948 Israel declares itself a state; Arabs/Palestinians flee and fighting begins

1949 Fighting over Israel ends temporarily

1956 Suez War – Israel, Britain, and France attack Egypt; United Nations intervenes and fighting ends temporarily

1964 Palestinian Liberation Organization (PLO) founded by Arab League, calling for destruction of Israel and Zionism; PLO gradually becomes an independent organization for different political factions with varying agendas

1967 Six-Day War – Israel defeats Syria and Egypt and occupies the Sinai Peninsula; Palestinians remain in refugee camps or immigrate to the United States or elsewhere

1970-71 Jordanian Civil War; King Hussein defeats Palestinian guerrillas; PLO invades Lebanon

1970 Terrorist activities begin, including commercial plane hijackings and the Palestinian massacre of Israeli athletes at the 1972 Olympics in Munich, Germany

1973 October War – Egyptian and Syrian troops attempt to reclaim territories seized by Israel in 1967; (United States assists Israel; Soviet Union assists Arab states)

1974 Yassar Arafat and his group, al-Fatah, assume leadership of PLO, gaining more respect and eventual U.N. recognition

1975-91 Civil War in Lebanon

1978 Camp David Accord – Egypt and Israel sign a peace treaty, with the United States as a witness, but conflicts between Palestinians and Israel and between Syria and Israel remain unresolved

1980-88 Iraq-Iran War – no real resolution of differences despite ending of hostilities

1981 President Anwar Sadat assassinated by Egyptian soldiers

1983-85 Israel withdraws from Lebanon, except for "security zone" in south

1987-93 The *Intifada*—Palestinian uprising against the Israeli occupation[27]
1988 Palestinian Declaration of Independence and recognition by the U.N. General Assembly, with the United States and Israel voting "no" with 26 abstentions
1990s Israelis and Palestinians begin the negotiations to bring about a self-governing Palestinian state
1990 Iraq invades Kuwait
1991 Gulf War – the United States, with the aid of Canada and a number of European and Arab nations, expels Iraqis from Kuwait
1992 Algerian Civil War
1993-on Increased terrorists activities in the Arab world and beyond, including attacks on the World Trade Center in New York in 1993 and September 11, 2001
2003 War in Iraq and aftermath; some progress made in resolving Arab-Israeli conflict.

Key Issues of Conflict in Arab World/Middle East

- The Jews trace their claim to Palestine back to the biblical kingdoms of Israel and Judah prior to Jerusalem's fall to Rome in A.D. 70, but the Palestinians, who have lived in Palestine for centuries, believe the land is rightfully theirs and desire self-determination and territorial sovereignty.

- Jerusalem is a city sacred to the world's three major religions. It is where the Jewish King Solomon built a great temple; it is the site of many events related to the life of Jesus; and it contains the Dome of the Rock mosque, the place from which, according to Islamic belief, the Prophet Muhammad ascended into heaven. In 1948 Jerusalem was divided into the Old City, under Jordan's control, and the New City, Israel's capital. In 1967 Israel took control of the Old City, as well.

- In addition to conflicts between Arab countries and Israel, there is disagreement between and within Arab countries on many other religious, ethnic, and boundary issues.

[27] The *Intifada* was a civilian uprising that involved activities such as refusing to pay taxes, boycotting Israeli products, and peaceful and violent demonstrations. The Israeli response included imposition of curfews, restriction of travel, and violent attacks on Palestinian homes. There was a second *Intifada* in September 2000 and what some call a third *Intifada* in September 2002 (Kuttab. "Third Intifada." Arabic Media Internet Network).

CHAPTER FOUR

When and Why Arabs Came to America and Later to California

THE FIRST Arabs/Muslims in America were African slaves brought as captives as early as 1733. Antonius Bishallany was the first publicly recognized Syrian immigrant, arriving in New York in 1854, but dying of tuberculosis several years later. Other occasional visitors have been identified and several Arabs arrived to assist the federal government with the experimental U.S. Camel Corps project that imported over 70 camels to help build and supply a western wagon route from Texas to California in 1856.[28] Subsequently, there have been three major waves of Arab immigration to America.

First Wave of Immigration

The first great wave of Arab immigration took place between the late 1870s and early 1940s.[29] Between 1880 and 1914, an estimated 100,000 Syrians arrived in America, most

---

[28] Lieutenant Edward Fitzgerald Beale (for whom Beale Air Force Base in Marysville, California, is named) was in charge of the project and Hadji Ali (nicknamed Hi Jolly because the Americans could not pronounce his name) was the chief camel driver on a Western expedition in June 1857. The outbreak of the Civil War led to the abandonment of the project. Some of the animals were shot by prospectors and hunters after escaping into the desert, but most were auctioned off at the Benicia Arsenal in California in 1864 for placement in zoos or circuses or for hauling hay and salt for miners in Nevada. The camel herd driven to Benicia in 1863 was pastured behind two of the Quarter Master's Buildings, thus the nickname Camel Barns, one of which houses a museum today. Hi Jolly kept a few of the camels and later started a freighting business in Arizona. The business failed, however, and Jolly released his last camel in the desert near Gila Bend. Years later, Hi Jolly moved to Quartzsite, Arizona, where he died in 1902. A memorial stands in his honor and Quartzsite holds a festival—"Hi Jolly Daze"—every year.

[29] The Joseph Arbeelys of Damascus were the first Syrian family to arrive in the United States in 1878 (Hitti 48).

Reference to Syrians

- At different times throughout its history, Syria has included parts of what are now Lebanon, Israel, Palestine, Jordan, Iraq, and Turkey. It was invaded, occupied, and colonized by many different races, religions, and empires. Thus the Syrians who came to America as early as the late 1870s were from a larger area than the Syria of today and represented many different racial backgrounds. The majority, however, were Arab in origin.

- When the national origins quota system was permanently instituted in 1924, allowing only two percent of the number of foreign-born persons of each nationality residing in the United States in 1890 to immigrate, the Arabs began dividing themselves into politically distinct groups of Syrians, Lebanese, Jordanians, and Palestinians.

- By the 1950s, the racial term "Arab" and the national term "Syrian" went out of vogue and most desired to be called "Lebanese." Understandably, the immigrants themselves were confused about their identity—especially those who arrived during the time of the Ottoman Empire and were listed as Turks. American-born children who successfully assimilated and adopted the American culture were impacted by confusion about their ancestry.

---

via Ellis Island. World War I (1914-18) slowed the migration, but a surge of Syrians who had survived wartime famine began arriving soon thereafter.

Between 1920 and 1924 more than 12,000 Syrians came to America. The Quota Act of 1921, the first immigration law to impose numerical limitations, again caused reductions in numbers, and was made permanent by Congress as the Johnson-Reed Immigration Act of 1924. Two other significant slow-downs during the first wave of immigration occurred during the Great Depression (1929-41) and World War II (1939-45).

Little is known about what triggered the first migration in the 1870s. No momentous political or economic event was taking place in any part of the Arab world at this time, although scholars have debated whether Christian Arabs came to escape oppression under the Turkish Ottoman Empire or as a result of the massacre in 1860 of 22,000 Christians in Zahle by the Druzes.

Several scholars believe that the call for arts and crafts exhibitors at the 1876 Centennial Exhibition in Philadelphia may have been the initial impetus. Entrepreneurs from such North African countries as Morocco, Algeria, Tunisia, and Egypt, as well as provinces of the Turkish Ottoman Empire like Syria, became aware of American prosperity for the first time and discovered a new market for their products—especially Holy Land curios that were coveted by Americans.

Some stayed on after the exhibition was over, but others returned home to share their newfound knowledge with family and friends—recommending that they join them in returning to seek a fortune in America. Subsequent fairs had the same effect—the Columbian Exposition in Chicago in 1893 and the St. Louis Fair in 1904.[30]

The three expositions also brought Syrian entertainers to America, many of whom remained afterwards, finding employment in circuses or in the theater. Some even joined "Buffalo Bill's Wild West" show (Younis 166), which no doubt exposed them to California and its desirable climate and agricultural land which would favor crops familiar to their families—olives, grapes, and oranges.

As early as the 1820s and '30s, the Arabs also learned about America through Protestant missionaries who began opening churches and schools and distributing missionary material in Syria. The Syrian Protestant College (today's

[30] At the St. Louis Fair, the ice cream cone was accidentally "invented" by a Syrian sugar-waffle concessionaire who came to the aid of an ice cream vendor when he ran out of ice cream plates. "The idea became an overnight sensation known as 'World's Fair Cornucopias.' By 1906, the shortened version of 'cones' took over in popularity" (Younis 164-165). Reputedly, the concessionaire was 18-year-old Fifie Malouf, later of Redondo Beach, California. See page 117 (Zahn letter).

American University of Beirut) was established in 1866; it trained much-needed doctors and other medical personnel. The American mission press also made a positive impression by producing and printing a new translation of the Bible in Arabic, as well as secular textbooks on Arabic grammar, algebra, geometry, and geography, all of which enhanced Syrian education.

The missionaries established a lasting bond between Syrians and Americans that fueled a Syrian desire to visit America. Few Muslims converted to Christianity under the American missionary period, but many were influenced by Western ideas and technology and also developed an interest in venturing to America.

In the midst of the Industrial Revolution and westward expansion, America was in need of cheap labor for factories, coal mines, and other industries, and also offered settlers the opportunity to occupy newly acquired lands. Manufacturers, railroads, state immigration bureaus, and steamship companies initiated publicity campaigns to recruit people from all parts of the world. The Arabic publishing community assisted in the effort by publishing promotional and informative articles about America (Naff *Becoming* 93; Younis 171).

The interest of some farmers was piqued by rumors that the President of the United States (Abraham Lincoln) was giving land away for free, which was true to an extent, as set forth in the Homestead Act of 1862. Generally, though, Syrians were not interested in establishing their own farms widely separated from any neighbors. They were accustomed to village life and living in close proximity to others (Harik 33).

Following the Civil War (1861-65), a number of Americans, including Mark Twain, Theodore Roosevelt, Sr., and his young son, Teddy, visited Syria on vacation or to assist the American missionaries (Younis 71). Guides and interpreters assisting the American travelers became sources of information about America for their family and friends.

The Ottomans first permitted emigration in the 1880s and '90s; any emigration previously had been on the sly. At this time the first wave of migration was also spurred by several economic setbacks for Syria and Mount Lebanon in the form of heavy taxation under the Ottoman Turks, a bacterial disease that infected vineyards, Chinese and Japanese competition in the Lebanese silk market,[31] Egyptian competition in the tobacco industry, and American competition (from Florida and California) in the citrus trade.

In 1908 the Ottoman government began drafting both Muslim and Christian Arabs into the Turkish army. This prompted many to migrate to avoid military service, including a few thousand Muslims and Druze. There was widespread fear that Arab soldiers were assigned hazardous duty in the Arabian deserts and most likely would never return home. Families rationalized that if their sons had to leave home it might as well be to enhance the family's finances rather than to risk their lives.

Muslims and Druze had previously been reluctant to try life in a Christian country fearing that they might not be accepted or that their beliefs and traditions might be diluted by external influences. Some of the early Muslim and Druze immigrants assumed Christian surnames and traveled and peddled with Christians. Meeting with success, they soon sent encouraging letters to friends and families back home, convincing them that life in a Christian country would not interfere with their religious practices (Naff *Arab Americans* 33).

With the defeat of the Turks at the end of World War I, there was political unrest and economic stagnation in the

[31] The opening of the Suez Canal in 1869 created a short cut to the Far East, making it easier for China and Japan to compete with the Syrian-Lebanese in the French market for silk.

Arab world. A plague of locusts struck in 1915, disease and hunger had devastated Syria and Lebanon during the war, and medicine and doctors were scarce.

Furthermore, much of the Arab world had come under British, French, and Italian influence with colonial governments, which caused considerable resentment. The Syrians also objected to the British pledge in the Balfour Declaration of 1917 to create a Jewish homeland on Arab Palestinian soil and seethed at the subsequent influx of European Jews to the area. Consequently, several hundred more Syrians immigrated to America and elsewhere in the world. However, with enactment of the Quota Act of 1924, Arab immigration was halted until after World War II, with the exception of Palestinians who qualified as refugees.[32]

Characteristics of the First Wave of Arab Immigrants

Most of the first immigrants were from then Syria—particularly Mount Lebanon, and most were Christians of the Eastern-rite sects—mainly Maronite, Melkite, or eastern Orthodox. Five to ten percent were Sunni or Shi'ite Muslims and a few were of the semi-Islamic Druze faith (Naff *Becoming American* 2).

The immigrants were small farmers, artisans, and skilled laborers of various trades—single men, fathers and sons, a few husbands and wives, and some wives without husbands. They intended to stay only a couple of years to take advantage of the moneymaking opportunities available working in the industrial factories and textile mills of the Northeast, or to become traveling dry goods "peddlers." Most were poor, but by pooling family resources—maybe even mortgaging their land—they were able to raise the $50 for steerage, train fare, and incidentals (Naff *Becoming American* 89-90).

[32] Once Jewish immigrants started resettling in Palestine, Arabs were edged out of landownership and business.

Peddling Across the U.S. to California

- Before the advent of the Sears-Roebuck catalogue in 1896, peddling was the primary means used to distribute goods to the rural areas of America.

- Peddling was not unique to Syrian immigrants—Irish, Germans, Scandinavians, Greeks, Italians, Armenians, and east European Jews peddled as well. Syrians were "back" peddlers, however, who carried their wares from town to town on their backs. The other immigrant peddlers usually conducted their business in the city from a pushcart.

- The Syrians also developed a unique network of settlements that ensured their success and eventual assimilation in America. The majority of Syrians came from small villages and, once in America, they connected with a network of settlements located primarily in the east and midwest, but also eventually on the west coast.

- Each settlement was headed by a merchandise supplier who handled everyone's finances, provided housing, briefed them on procedures, and organized the peddling distribution routes. Goods were restocked through shipments via parcel post or express delivery, and receiving stations were set up in certain areas (Younis 126). By the first decade of the 20th century, there were several business directories published for networking purposes.

- A remarkable number of Christian Syrian women immigrated alone to either join their husbands, marry their fiances, or peddle on their own, some having left their husbands behind. If Syrian wives did not peddle themselves, they made small articles of clothing or perhaps Syrian bread and sweets for their husbands to sell.

- The first peddled merchandise consisted of holy items like rosaries, crosses, or religious icons displayed on a stick. Americans were enthralled that these people were from the Holy Land and assumed that all of their merchandise must be blessed. The peddlers soon acquired small notions cases (*kashshi*) that they filled with whatever sewing needs would fit in the small drawers. This led to the sale of fabrics, ribbons, linens, laces, underwear, shirts, socks, garters, suspenders, and gloves and caps, as well as a variety of toiletries, women's accessories, and bric-a-brac—picture frames, mirrors, and other household

Peddling Across the U.S. to California (Continued)

decorative items. (Women peddlers often were more successful than men because they seemed more skilled at selling the items that American housewives particularly wanted.)

- Backpacks supported by shoulder straps weighed over 100 pounds. When buggies, and later, automobiles became available, peddlers began to stock heavy Oriental rugs.

- The arrival of Syrian women soon led to the loss of appeal of the peddler lifestyle. Syrians established households and became permanent citizens of the United States. Many Americanized their Arab names that were difficult to pronounce and spell since Arabic sounds are not found in English (Naff *Arab Americans* 65).

- Peddlers provided an invaluable service to America (that probably was not recognized at the time) in the following ways:

  - Brought needed household items to remote parts of the country and were willing to barter when a customer was short on cash. In this way they promoted commerce where money was scarce. Farmers' wives were their best customers.

  - Expanded the markets of small American industries, thus increasing the production levels and profitability of American companies.

  - Prolonged the vocation of peddling despite the advancements and changes brought about by the Industrial Revolution. As a result, during the Great Depression, it was easy for thousands of proud and desperate people to take up peddling as a way to avoid jobless-ness and demoralization (Naff *Becoming American* 125). Through ingenuity and hard work, many were able to provide at least a subsistence living for their families.

Adapted from Naff (*Becoming American* and *Arab Americans*) and Younis

The peddlers met the needs of a unique niche market of housewives and non-English speaking immigrants living in urban neighborhoods, industrial and mining towns, or on farms. Consequently, they prospered financially and also became comfortable with American ways, so few returned to their homeland, except temporarily.[33] Many

[33] The San Francisco Farrah family (See page 88.) recounts an interesting story about

sold their farms and vineyards or paid off their mortgages in order to provide support to churches or mosques or to relatives who remained behind (Naff *Becoming American* 114).

Once back in America, they often started their own businesses and helped family members and friends join them. Eventually word of the wealth to be made in America spread among extended families and, by the 1880s, a chain migration was well under way.

An elaborate network system of services was initially developed for the peddling trade, but eventually was used by all Syrians immigrating to America. The system put the travelers at ease, reduced the number of mishaps during transit from the homeland, and provided living accommodations in settlements that sprang up across the country.[34] Most new arrivals knew exactly where they were going and how they would earn their anticipated wealth. The network system also served as a communications link between the homeland and America. Immigrants placed complete reliance on it until fraud and deception corrupted it. By 1910 Syrians had become savvy enough to handle their relocation arrangements individually (Naff *Becoming American* 94-95, 106).

During the period of railroad building, with long and short lines branching in all directions throughout the United States, the Syrians followed the railroads, not as laborers, but as merchants. It was the Syrian-Lebanese peddlers who eventually made it to California by the 1880s. Traveling by train across the country, they passed through California and

---

one such return trip. In 1928 George Farrah and his recently widowed cousin, Andrew J.Andrew, a farmer from Turlock, returned to Lebanon and Syria on a "mating trip." The end result was two "whirlwind courtships," weddings a week apart, and the return of the two couples to California on the same ship.

[34]Teckla Malouf operated such settlements, first in Los Angeles in the 1890s, and then in Niagara Falls, New York in the early 1900s, where she ran a rooming house that was a center for immigrant relatives and fellow countrymen from Zahle, Lebanon. (See page 114 for more about Teckla Malouf.)

were enamored with California's climate and natural environment that was so similar to their homeland, as well as the opportunities available in farming and merchandising. Word soon reached farmers in Syria and Lebanon and they began heading for the agricultural areas of the state, especially the San Joaquin Valley.

Many Yemenis (mostly Muslims) came to California to work as farmers or migrant farm workers. For the most part their wives and children remained in Yemen and they sent one-half of their income home to them. During World War I some Yemenis joined the U.S. Army, became U.S. citizens, and after the war started their own businesses.

In areas throughout the western United States receiving settlers from the east and mid-west, as well as immigrants from all over the world, there was a dire need for dry goods and grocery stores. The Syrian-Lebanese responded by opening family businesses in which all members of the family worked. Others established factories that manufactured clothing (especially lingerie, Japanese kimonos, gloves, and hats), as well as silk and linen fabrics. These independent, enterprising, hard-working people were willing to move wherever opportunity beckoned.

Second Wave of Immigration

The second great wave of Arab immigration began when colonialism formally came to an end after World War II. Several new independent Arab nations were created, or in some areas, military regimes took control, posing as republics or monarchies supported by the former colonial powers.

People from many other parts of the Arab world besides Syria and Lebanon sought refuge from the prevailing political upheaval, especially the Palestinians[35] after the formation

[35] Passage of the Refugee Relief Act of 1953 and its extension in 1957 led to large numbers of Palestinians entering the U.S. in 1953 and also between 1958 and 1963.

Unreliable Population Statistics

It is difficult to accurately trace Arab immigration to the United States or to estimate the size of the current Arab American population for a number of reasons:

- Most Arab immigrants arriving in America before World War II were not classified accurately by the Bureau of Immigration.
- Americans have always been confused about who people from Arabic-speaking countries are. They have been referred to as Turks, Syrians, Arabs, Arabians, Muslims, Syrian-Lebanese, Palestinians, Asians, Turks in Asia, Greeks, Armenians, Assyrians, Caucasians, and noted variously as white, black, and colored.
- In 1899 the Bureau of Immigration began to compile data by race as well as by country of birth or origin. Thus the classification of "Syrian" was added to its records so that they could be distinguished from the Turks and Armenians also coming from the Ottoman Empire. The term "Palestinian" started being used later, and even today some Palestinians are counted as Jordanians because they are refugees and carry passports from the West Bank, which was under Jordanian rule from 1948-1967.
- The 1910 census continued to include the Syrians and Palestinians under the category "Turks in Asia." Even today, Arab immigrants, including Palestinians, are often classified as "other Asian" or "other African."
- In recent years, immigration officials have registered Arab immigrants according to their last country of residence, which could have been a non-Arab European country, Canada, or South or Central America. Even the 2000 Census did not count Arabs separately in the race or ethnicity question (they are considered Caucasian or white), but the long form did include an ancestry question, so at least the third generation Arab Americans could identify their Arab grandparents.
- Census data classify two Christian groups of immigrants by distinctive ancestries, not as Arabs. One group is the people of Assyrian or Chaldean ancestry—a large Catholic group from Iraq. The other group consists of Christian Armenians who probably reported their ancestry as Armenian rather than the Arabic-speaking country from which they migrated (Haddad and Smith 136).   (Continued)

32

Unreliable Population Statistics (Continued)

- Many of the earliest Syrian immigrants departed their homeland with the help of a network of services that took care of making all the arrangements for passage to America, finding employment, housing, etc. However, the system misrouted hundreds of people to South America instead of their intended United States destination where their friends and families resided. Sometimes, decades later, the determined ones finally reached the United States not as Syrians, but as Brazilians or Argentinians or Mexicans (Naff *Becoming American* 98). Even after 1965 with the change in immigration law, many of the Latin American and Asian immigrants were in fact Arabs who had earlier migrated to those two areas of the world.

- Arabs traveled frequently to and from their homeland to marry or meet family and financial obligations. Until immigration regulations were reformed in 1893, many of these entries were counted more than once, especially if the temporary return to the homeland was extended for a number of years.

- Many Arabs entered the United States on student visas and stayed after completing their education without being accounted for. Later, the professional-preference clause in the U.S. Immigration and Nationality Act of 1965 allowed many Arab professionals to immigrate legally.

- During the early 20th century when there was a surge of "nativism" (the policy of perpetuating native cultures) in the United States and many restrictions were placed on immigration and citizenship for people from Eastern Europe and the Ottoman Empire, many Arabs tried to conceal their heritage. And, today, because of a cultural reluctance to share personal information with the government and because of a new prejudice against Arabs related to fears about terrorism, some Arab immigrants have deliberately falsified their country of origin. Others have slipped undetected across the Canadian and Mexican borders or crossed illegally via smuggling rings.

of the Jewish state of Israel in 1948 and the brief war that followed. Other upheavals included the toppling of Arab monarchies in Egypt in 1952, Iraq in 1958, Yemen in 1962, and Libya in 1969, as well as the Suez War in 1956.

Some were escaping the economic problems facing their new states, while others were participating in Arab state-sponsored economic development programs that included opportunities for technical, financial, and managerial training for Arab citizens in American educational institutions. Many students stayed after marrying an American citizen or through sponsorship of their American employer.

Some came to take advantage of career opportunities in professions for which they already had degrees—lawyers, doctors, and engineers. The earning potential and professional opportunities were much better in the United States than in most Arab countries. Others were sponsored by members of their families who were already U.S. citizens.

The second wave of over 300,000 Arabs was predominantly Muslim and most intended to stay only temporarily—just long enough to improve their economic status, receive training, and/or avoid the strife and dangers of the political conflicts and civil wars that they hoped would soon end. Unfortunately, the conflicts have continued and modernization did not advance rapidly enough to provide the jobs at home for which they were trained in the United States. Many highly educated young Arabs decided not to return home and even those who did ended up returning to the U.S. later in large numbers.

The discovery of the Arab world's oil reserves[36] and subsequent involvement of foreigners, including Americans, in the development of the reserves may have affected migration, as well. The influx of foreigners in the Arab oil-rich countries and exposure to Western culture and commodities from all parts of the world stimulated a yearning to migrate in pursuit of economic opportunities, political freedom, and a better way of life.

[36] Oil was struck in 1927 in Iraq, 1932 in Bahrain, 1936 in Saudi Arabia, 1938 in Kuwait, 1939 in Qatar, and 1964 in Oman.

Third Wave of Immigration

The third great wave of immigration occurred in the mid-1960s and continues today. Initially, the surge was due to the passage of the U.S. Immigration and Nationality Act of 1965, which abolished the quota system and its bias against non-European immigration.[37] The immigration of Arabs peaked between 1968 and 1971, following the defeat of Egypt, Syria, and Jordan by Israel in the Six-Day War of 1967. However, the immigration has remained constant due to the intermittent warfare and constant political tension and economic hardships that have troubled this region. In fact, many countries have been sending students to the United States to gain expertise in economic development and many have chosen to remain here.

There were wars in 1973, 1980, 1982, 1990, the Gulf War in 1991, and the war in Iraq in 2003; coups in Syria, Libya, Iraq, and Sudan; wars of independence in Algeria, Tunisia, and Palestine; and long periods of civil war in Algeria, Sudan, Yemen, Lebanon, and Iraq. Several countries have been subject to missile and bombing raids by the United States in retaliation for terrorist attacks on American embassies and ships. Still other countries like Sudan have suffered from drought, famine, and rampant disease, as well as civil strife ignited by the country's militant Islamic regime.

Even the 1979 Islamic-led revolution in Iran, a non-Arab country, caused some Arabs to migrate from their countries. With the overthrow of the conservative, pro-Western monarchy of the Shah of Iran, many in neighboring Arab countries feared the outbreak of Islamic revolutions in their countries. The subsequent Iraq-Iran War only added to this fear.

The entire war-torn Arab world is politically unstable and suffers from unchecked population growth, housing

---

[37] It is estimated that more than 400,000 Arabs arrived in the U.S. between 1965 and 1992.

shortages, some of the highest rates of unemployment in the world, urban poverty, income inequalities, and a growth of Islamic fundamentalism that is fomenting terror throughout the world, but particularly within the Arab world. The governments of most Arab countries lack public support or participation. Most states serve the interests of the elite and ignore the needs of the average citizen (Gerner 267).

The latest wave of Arab immigrants has included professionals[38] and entrepreneurs of all kinds, as well as unskilled and semi-skilled laborers—most with their immediate families in tow. They settle wherever they can find jobs, with some professionals resorting to employment as clerks, cab drivers, or waiters out of necessity. Others have become owners of hotels, restaurants, bakeries, supermarkets, tobacco and speciality food stores; gas stations and convenience stores, auto dealerships and repair shops, import/export companies, stationery stores, or real estate, insurance, and travel agencies. Many work in the high-tech industry, both as technicians or owners of high-tech companies, and many others are teachers or college professors. All are seeking economic opportunities and respite from undesirable conditions in their homeland.

Some Arab Americans send a significant amount of their earnings ("remittances") back to their homelands to support family members who remain there. In several countries these monies account for one of the largest cash flows of their economies. The Moroccan government actually encourages emigration abroad in order to reduce unemployment and reap the benefit of the workers' income sent home to their families (Wilkins 77).

---

[38] Many Arab professionals were able to enter the U.S. under the terms of a professional-preference clause in the Immigration and Naturalization Act of 1965 based on educational qualifications. Emigration continues to be an attractive option because professional jobs and commensurate salaries are lacking in the Arab world.

California's Arab Americans

The 1990 Census figures for Californians who reported at least one specific ancestry group cited a total of 8,786 from the Arab world region. However, this figure is meaningless because it does not include thousands of Arab Americans for a number of reasons. (See pages 31-32.)[39]

The largest concentration of Arab Americans is in Los Angeles,[40] but other large populations are found in San Diego, Orange County, Santa Barbara, San Francisco and the surrounding Bay Area, and Sacramento. Many arrivals since 1967 came to California to continue their education, and following graduation, gravitated to the existing Arab communities in the urban areas of the state, especially in Southern California. Some have established new Arab communities in urban areas, such as the Egyptian Coptic (Christian) settlement in Los Angeles.

The first immigrants to arrive in California were Syrian and Lebanese, but today the majority of Arab Americans in California are Egyptian and Palestinian (especially in the San Francisco Bay Area). Others, many of whom have over-stayed their student visas, are from Morocco, Yemen, and Algiers. There are many Chaldeans and Assyrians from Iraq, but they do not consider themselves Arab Americans.[41]

[39] The 1990 Census record breakdown: Algeria 64; Arab 1,725; Egyptian 588; Iraqi 202; Jordanian 235; Lebanese 3,784; Moroccan 97; Palestinian 451; Saudi Arabian 185; Syrian 1,189; Yemeni 32; and other North Africa and Southwest Asia 234.

[40] In recent years Los Angeles moved ahead of Detroit as the U.S. urban area with the highest concentration of Arab Americans. Weather similar to many Arab countries and employment opportunities are the lure of Los Angeles.

[41] The fairly large Assyrian-Chaldean population primarily from Iraq is centered in

In the 1960s, a chain migration of young Yemeni men began in the Stockton and Delano areas that continued into the 1970s. Yemenis gradually replaced the Filipinos who had previously made up a large part of the migrant workforce. The economic boom in the oil-producing countries in the Persian Gulf lured many Yemenis back home in the late 1970s, but following the Gulf War, they returned to California. The farmworkers travel in groups throughout the farming regions of the state in accordance with the various harvest seasons for grapes in the Delano/Porterville area, asparagus in Stockton, Tracy, and Richgrove; cherries in Sunnyvale, plums in Shafter, and carrots in Holtville. Some travel to Marysville, Woodland, Salinas, and Indio to harvest other crops. The Yemenis may be joined by farm workers from Morocco, Egypt, Jordan, or Lebanon, as well.

Some of these farm workers, as their English improves, eventually move to urban areas such as Oakland, San Francisco, Bakersfield, and Fresno to obtain unskilled labor jobs or establish their own small businesses, especially grocery stores. If successful, many then send for their families to join them in making a new life here (Friedlander, ed. Kelley 69; Zogby, ed. Matalka 83, 85).

A large number of California's Arab Americans are third generation transplants from other parts of the country. Born in the United States of immigrant parents or grandparents, they moved to California to attend college, pursue professional job opportunities, fulfill military assignments at California military bases during the Vietnam War, or follow other family members who found the state to be a good place to live and work and raise a family.

Los Angeles, San Jose, Turlock, Modesto, and San Diego. This group will be discussed in the forthcoming book, *California: An International Community*.

CHAPTER SIX

North Coast Arab Americans

EUREKA, LOCATED on Humboldt Bay, has the largest port between San Francisco and Portland. It has been a major lumbering and fishing center since the 1850s. The Northwestern Railroad did not reach Eureka from San Francisco until 1914, but that did not deter Davis and Amelia Schemoon from arriving there in 1896 with their three children—George, Alfred, and Mary. They arrived from San Francisco on the steam schooner *Pomona*.

Davis had been among some of the first Syrians to arrive in the United States in 1887. A Maronite Christian from Zahle, Lebanon, he arrived with letters of introduction provided by American Presbyterian missionaries he met while attending the American University of Beirut. Educated and fairly fluent in English, Davis was invited to join the Chautauqua traveling lecture series in upstate New York—speaking about the Arabic language, as well as the customs, religious history, and geography of his homeland.

Davis Schemoon Family
in Eureka circa 1918
Courtesy of Jerry Colivas

In 1890 Davis moved to San Francisco where he bought a house on Telegraph Hill for $900.[42] Within a year, he sent for his wife, Amelia, in Lebanon, and they soon began their family. In 1896 a Syrian acquaintance of the Schemoon's living in Humboldt County praised the North Coast as a highly desirable place to live; soon the Schemoon family was aboard the *Pomona* on their way to start a new life in Eureka, California.

Davis peddled clothes and various sundries between Eureka and Blue Lake, 20 miles to the northeast. He eventually bought a team of horses and a wagon so he could expand his territory another 40 miles to Hoopa, further to the northeast.

In 1907 Davis opened a clothing store at Second and Y streets in Eureka. In 1912 he closed this store so he could open another one closer to town. Because his son, George, was working for him by then, the store at Second and E streets was called Davis Schemoon and Son. George joined the U.S. Army during World War I and was sent to France. The store closed soon after the war ended in 1918.

In 1922 Davis opened his first grocery store and in 1926, a second one, which George operated. Davis delivered groceries to his customers using the team of horses and wagon that he had used in peddling.

Davis Schemoon and Son clothing store at Second and E streets in Eureka - Courtesy of Jerry Colivas

[42]The house remains today and is valued at close to a million dollars, however, the Schemoon family no longer owns it.

In the meantime, between 1900 and 1912, five more children were added to the Schemoon household—Joseph, Kelly, William, Amelia, and Edward. Kelly was permanently disabled in an accident while helping his father deliver groceries; their team of horses was startled by the sounds of the streetcars on Broadway. Kelly was seriously injured when he was thrown from the wagon. In adulthood he became a street peddler, selling various sundries out of a drawer from this wheelchair. He died at the age of 36.

When Davis retired, George and Edward each took over a store. Davis died in Eureka in 1935; relatives and friends came from as far away as Lebanon to attend the funeral. George's store burned down in the 1930s and Edward closed his in 1942 when he left Eureka to enlist in the U.S. Army. The other family members moved to San Francisco during World War II.

One of Davis and Amelia's grandsons, Jerry Colivas, the son of Mary Schemoon Colivas, was born in Eureka in 1925. Jerry grew up in San Francisco, but returned to Eureka in 1951, after serving in the U.S. Army during World War II and attending college. He served as principal of Eureka High School during the 1970s.

In retirement Jerry enjoys writing about the history of Humboldt County. His article, entitled "'A Good Businessman'- Davis Schemoon Becomes an Integral Part of Downtown Eureka," appeared in the Spring 2000 issue of *Humboldt Historian* magazine and provided the facts for the foregoing account of the Schemoon family. Jerry's life story was once featured on Eureka's local Public Broadcasting Service television station.

Today only a handful of Arab Americans live in the North Coast area of California, primarily in Mendocino County. There are no known Eastern-rite Christian churches or mosques, nor are there any Middle Eastern restaurants—all usually good indicators of a sizeable Arab American population.

Arab American Family Structure

- It is difficult to generalize about the family characteristics of Arab Americans because there are many variables, including country of origin, whether the family came from a rural or urban region, religion, length of time in the United States, degree of assimilation, economic and educational status, and individual characteristics.
- Traditionally, Arab families were large and extended families lived together. Marriages occurred at a young age, in-group marriages were encouraged to preserve cultural heritage, children were named according to Christian and Muslim traditions, and women were subservient to men. But today, even in the Arab world, progress is being made to eliminate the gender gap for women in their roles outside the home and to provide more leadership opportunities for women in their communities.
- For Muslim families, Islam teaches that men and women are equal but different. Men are responsible for financially supporting their families and women are responsible for raising the children and running the household. Generally, women who want to work outside the home are free to do so, but they must also perform their family duties.
- Today there are many variations of these traditions, and families who have been in America for many years—Christian and Muslim families alike—are very Americanized. One characteristic that remains universal, however, is that most Arabs retain a loyal attachment to their families. The ability of Arab families to work together and support one another is the secret behind their success. Even when families live in different parts of the world, they are expected to help each other financially and socially.
- Arabs believe in a strong work ethic and traditionally place a high priority on education for their children. Parental sacrifices to ensure the best possible education are commonplace.

CHAPTER SEVEN

Shasta Cascade Arab Americans

IN THE NORTHEAST corner of Modoc County, in north-eastern California, Fort Bidwell was established in 1865 to protect pioneer settlers in the area from the Native Americans unhappy with the presence of Euro-Americans. Abandoned as a military post in 1893, it then was used as a government school for Native Americans until 1930. A small town called Fort Bidwell developed in Surprise Valley.

The 1939-40 issue of the *Syrian Directory of the State of California* lists Shaheen Santiago operating a general merchandise store in Fort Bidwell. Unable to locate any-one familiar with the Santiago family, one can only surmise that maybe they passed through the area on the Nevada-California-Oregon Railway (NCO) while peddling across the country and were told that two stores were thriving in Fort Bidwell—Kober's and Lowell's. The 1932 "Modoc County Index of Registered Voters, Ft. Bidwell Precinct," lists four Santiagos—Sandy, a merchant; Ida E., a housewife; Mitchell, a clerk; and Adele M., a clerk (Brown 5 Apr. 2003).

Approximately 50 miles south of Fort Bidwell in Alturas, George and Claire Arabold opened a dry goods store on Main Street shortly before 1920. They had three daughters—Josephine, Mary, and Lucille (Morgan 9 Apr. 2003).

To the west, Weed, in Siskiyou County, had a booming logging and lumber industry in the early 1900s, which attracted a few Lebanese, some of whom eventually moved to the San Francisco Bay Area.

Both the 1939-40 and 1948-50 Syrian-Lebanese directories list the Clifford Bourestom, Samuel Ganim, and Albert

Mussallam families as residents of Weed. (See below about the Bourestoms and Ganims.) Albert Mussallam was a tailor. Today only descendants of the Ganim family remain in Weed. They are related to a long-time Arab American family in Redding.

Redding, founded in 1872, has always been a center of trade and transportation, with roads leading east and west, north and south, and the Southern Pacific Railroad passing through on its way to Oregon since the 1880s. It is likely that the railroad is how the Lebanese family of Joseph Solomon Ganim ("Ghanem" before the name was Americanized) arrived in Redding at the turn of the 20th century. Joseph sold garden produce from a horse drawn wagon around town, eventually traveling as far as Weaverville, 45 miles west of Redding, and expanding his sales to hardware and clothing. On one of his trips to Weaverville, he must have heard about the gold still being mined in Whiskeytown, because he soon established Ganim Gold Mines, Inc. This successful gold mining company had its own steam powered stamp mill and 20 employees; it continued in operation until the 1940s.

Joseph and Sadie Ganim circa 1900

In his later years, Joseph farmed an acre of this property using what he called "old country" farming methods to get the most out of every inch. He canned his fruits and vegetables and made his own wine from the grapes. He also had 11 goats, and from the goat's milk he made white, piquant cheese, using an old Lebanese recipe (Luby *Redding Record-Searchlight*).

Joseph and Sadie had three children. When their two sons, Philip and Samuel, became young adults, they both headed off for greener pastures in Los Angeles and Hawaii. Eventually they returned to the Shasta Cascade area to open businesses and raise their own families. (Note: Sadie Ganim died of "dropsy" in 1915, so Joseph no doubt was pleased to have his family return home. He called his farm in the country his "bachelor home." Joseph died in 1960 at the age of 84.)

Joseph Ganim circa 1940

Philip had a photo studio in Dunsmuir, owned the Cascade Hotel and several apartment buildings in Redding, and developed homesites west of Redding. Today his three daughters, Marie, Vickie, and Sandra, live in other parts of California.

Samuel met and married Emmilene Bourestom while in Los Angeles. Her family was from Lebanon, as well. While visiting Joseph one summer, a move to Redding was discussed, but in Emmilene's opinion, Redding was too hot. Joseph suggested that Weed, at a higher elevation, would be cooler. The family took a drive there and Emmilene liked it; soon thereafter they moved to Weed.

Bonnie, Phil, Sam, Emmilene, Joseph & Joe Ganim

The young couple started out selling dresses out of the back of their car to the cooks, wives, and other women living in the logging camps in the area. Eventually they opened Ganim's Dress Shop in Weed. In 1949 they sold the dress shop to Emmilene's uncle, Clifford Bourestom, and opened Ganim's Mens and Boys Shop.

In the mid-1960s Sam and Emmilene sold the building where their clothing store was located. At the same time, the State of California bought their residential property for the Interstate-5 right-of-way. The Ganims moved to Redding—into a house with air conditioning. Their son, Joe, remains in Weed today, and their daughter, Bonnie, lives in Morgan Hill. There are six grandchildren and 12 great grand-children on this side of the family.

Finally, Joseph and Sadie's daughter, Edna, also an adventurer, worked in San Francisco for awhile and then went to Cairo, Egypt to visit her aunt. Here she met her future husband, a Royal Air Force en- listee, Donald Bracken.

Edna Ganim circa 1918-20

Edna and young Philip Bracken in Egypt

The Brackens began raising their two sons in England and Egypt, until Donald retired from the RAF in 1948.

The family moved to Redding and established a nursery, Bracken Gardens, that remains in business today as Bracken Garden Center. Their son, Philip, lives in Shasta, west of Redding; their other son, Donald, died in 1988.

(Family history and photographs courtesy of Philip Bracken and Joe Ganim.)

Another longtime Arab American family in Redding is the Michael J. ("Mike") and Sarah Naify Kassis family. Mike was born in North Dakota and was part of the Charles and Sophie Kassis family who immigrated to America from Lebanon in the first decade of the 20th century and eventually ended up in Sacramento. (See page 52.) Sarah Naify Kassis was part of the Naify family who arrived in California around 1916. (See pages 48, 53, 82, 91, and 95 for more about the Naify family.)

Mike entered the theater business via Sarah's brother, Michael A. Naify, who was president and general manager of T. & D., Jr. Enterprises, a movie theater chain. (See page 95.) Mike worked at the Metropolitan Theater in San Francisco for three years before requesting a transfer to Redding, where he became manager of the Redding Theatre.

At Mike's suggestion, T. & D., Jr. Enterprises built the upscale Cascade Theatre in downtown Redding in 1935. Mike managed this luxurious art deco theater for its first 31 years and provided employment for many Redding teenagers, including his own three children, Barbara, Raymond, and Robert.

Mike, along with a partner, also operated the Army/Navy Surplus stores located in Redding, Project City, Anderson,

and Red Bluff for many years. Raymond joined his father in that business, Robert worked as a civil engineer for the California Department of Transportation, and Barbara was a school teacher. All three children each had three children of their own. Raymond and Robert still live in Redding today and Barbara lives in Red Bluff.

(Family history courtesy of Raymond and Robert Kassis and Barbara Kassis Moses.)

Cascade Theatre in Redding circa 1940s
Courtesy of the Shasta Historical Society

Four Ayoob brothers arrived in America from Mt. Lebanon around 1908, leaving their diseased vineyards behind. George Ayoob moved to Los Angeles, but the other three brothers—Saul, Mike, and Tom—made their way to San Francisco. Before long, the three brothers headed for Plumas County, southeast of Redding.

Plumas County had been a hot bed of gold mining activity along the Feather River since the early days of the Gold Rush, and quartz-mining

Tom Ayoob, Sr. Family 1910

operations continued until the 1930s and '40s in some areas. Copper mines and lumber mills were also attracting families to the area looking for work and a nice place to raise their children. Around 1900 the Western

Tom Ayoob, Sr. Family

Pacific Railroad began passing through the area, as well, making travel to the area easier.

The three Ayoob brothers started out peddling yardage, trim, and notions in a horse and buggy in the Sierra and Indian valleys. They would be away from home for two weeks at a time, staying at ranch houses along the way. Saul died around 1919; Mike opened the first Ayoob Brother's clothing store in Greenville around 1920; and Tom opened another store in Quincy in 1921. Various family members later opened

Nick Ayoob

(Family history courtesy of Nicholas Ayoob. Photographs courtesy of John Cullen/Ayoob Family/Plumas County Museum.)

other stores in Chester, Portola, and Lovelock, Nevada. The stores in Quincy and Chester remain in operation today. Tom's son, Nicholas, and grandchildren and great-grandchildren of both brothers remain in the area.

One Syrian-Lebanese family, the Farris', was listed as residents of Susanville, in northeastern Plumas County in the 1948-50 directory. However, no details about this family were discovered.

To the southwest, in Butte County, Chico had been a thriving community since its founding in 1860 by John Bidwell—one of the first Americans to arrive in California in 1841. By 1921 Chico had a state teachers' college that subsequently became California State University, Chico.

In 1928, T. & D., Jr. Enterprises, one of the earliest theater chains in California, built the luxurious art deco Senator Theatre in Chico. T. & D. was owned by the two oldest brothers of the San Francisco-Syrian-Lebanese Naify family, and their younger brother Fred became the manager of the Chico theater. He continued as the manager until 1946, when he moved his family to Sacramento. Another brother, Lee, managed this theater at one time, as well. (See pages 45, 53, 82, 91, and 95 for further details about Fred's family and other branches of the Naify family.)

A significant Arab American population never developed in Chico, although there may be some who attend CSUC. There are no Eastern-rite sect churches or Middle Eastern restaurants, but there is one Islamic center, which may or may not have a significant number of Arab Americans associated with it.

Arab Cuisine

- Arab food is varied, but has some staples. Wheat is used in bread, pastries, salads, and main dishes, and rice is often cooked with vegetables, lamb, chicken, beef, or fish.
- Lamb is the most common meat eaten; pork is forbidden by Islam. Many Christian Arabs also avoid pork, but this is for cultural reasons.
- Arab recipes use many beans and vegetables, including eggplant, zucchini, and chickpeas.
- *Hummous*, a puree of chickpeas and oil, is a popular appetizer; dates and *baklava* (sticky mixture of syrup, honey, and nuts) are popular desserts.
- Coriander is the chief spice used, along with ginger, hot peppers, pimento, cumin, mint, cinnamon, onions, garlic, cloves, and parsley.
- The flat circular bread, which Americans call *pita* bread, is eaten with nearly every meal.
- Muslims are prohibited from drinking alcohol, so coffee and mint tea are favorite after-dinner drinks. The traditional preparation of coffee is a symbol of Arab hospitality.
- Most Arab countries have their own favorite dishes. Examples include:

    Algeria—firm and dense *couscous* (made by partially baking a coarsely ground durum wheat with water, then grinding it into a fine grain) served with lamb or chicken in a bed of cooked vegetables, *tabouleh* (a dish made of cracked wheat, parsley, tomato, mint, lemon, and spring onions), and *hummous* .

    Egypt—*moussaka* (a baked dish of layers of vegetables alternating with layers of minced meat and sauces) and *koshari* (lentils and rice topped with fried onion).

    Jordan—*mansaf* (lamb seasoned with herbs, cooked in yogurt, and served with rice), *shish kebab* (barbecued chunks of lamb and vegetables threaded onto skewers), and *shawarma* (a rolled piece of flat bread filled with strips of lamb or chicken).

    Lebanon—*baba ghanoush* (spiced, baked, or char-grilled eggplant served as a dip) and *shish kebabs* (skewered chunks of meat or fish cooked over charcoal).

    Libya—*shakshouka* (a dish of chopped lamb and tomato sauce) and *babaghanoug* (a paste of sesame seeds and mashed eggplant seasoned with spices).

    Saudi Arabia—*falafel* (deep fried balls of ground chickpeas and herbs) and *shawarma* (a sandwich of roast meat and pickled vegetables).

    Syria—*bulgar* (wheat that has been boiled, dried, and crushed), *mezze* (appetizers), and *tabouleh*. (See Algeria.)

    Tunisia—*harrissa* (spicy paste made of ground dried chilies, spices, garlic, and olive oil served as a side dish).

    United Arab Emirates— *mezze*, *kibbe* (meatballs), *hummous*, *tabouleh*, and *tahini* (paste made from sesame seeds).

- Arab cuisine has become Americanized and popularized and may be sampled and enjoyed at restaurants generally listed under Middle Eastern or Mediterranean cuisine.

Note: In 2002 California enacted legislation aimed at curbing consumer fraud among food producers and sellers claiming to have *halal* foods. Businesses must disclose that they are indeed providing *halal* food to their customers. The term "halal" means that which Allah and the Prophet Muhammad have allowed to be done in a lawful manner. Products must be slaughtered and prepared in accordance with Islamic dietary laws.

CHAPTER EIGHT

Gold Country and Sacramento Valley
Arab Americans

THE DISCOVERY of gold in Coloma in 1848 led to the first significant influx of immigrants to California, particularly to the Gold Country, from many parts of the world,[43] but not the Arab world. According to the 1939-40 issue of the *Syrian Directory of the State of California*, there were only two Syrian-Lebanese families in the Gold Country; it could not be determined exactly how early they arrived.

Louis Fahily was a shoemaker in San Andreas in Calaveras County in 1940. He was married three times, but never had any children of his own. He helped his first wife, presumed from death records to have been the American-born Jannette Harney Fahily, raise her two daughters, Myrna and Elvina. Today there are two small streets in San Andreas named after them that tie into Fahily Circle, another short street where Louie's home was located.

A stepson of Louie's from his third marriage barely knew Louie, but he believes "he made shoes for folks working for the Work Projects Administration (WPA) in Calaveras County during the depression." Therefore, it is possible that Louie had been in San Andreas since the early 1920s. He apparently was active in the Shriners before passing away in Stockton in 1985 (Winkler 3 June 2003).

According to the same 1939-40 directory, George Farrah was operating the Grass Valley Orphanage. Mount St. Mary's Convent and Orphan Asylum in Grass Valley had been in

---

[43]See Janice Marschner's *California 1850 – A Snapshot in Time* and *California: An International Community* (2004 expected publication date) to learn more about immigration to California during the Gold Rush.

operation since 1866, and it is conceivable that another orphanage was needed as many children were orphaned in those days when hardrock gold miners who worked below ground were accidentally killed on the job. However, no details about the "Grass Valley Orphanage" or George Farrah were discovered.

The 1939-40 directory lists another Syrian-Lebanese shoemaker in the Gold Country—the Northern Mines region in Yuba City. According to several issues of the city directory, Ed Maloof had a shop located at a number of different locations between 1938 and 1942, including Fifth Street in 1942.

According to the 1948-50 Syrian-Lebanese directory, Roseville in Placer County was the home of Monte Joseph and Sam J. Zien, a policeman. Not far away in Elverta in Sacramento County, the earlier 1939-40 issue of the directory lists Fred Zine as a cement worker, Joseph Zine as a rancher, and Mike Zine as a carpenter. Others with the surnames Zine and Zien were also living in Sacramento this early, and both families have descendants living in both Placer and Sacramento counties today. Joe Zine, believed to be the Elverta rancher, also owned a grocery store on E Street in Sacramento as early as 1939.

By 1948-50 Fred Zine had acquired a grocery store on Del Paso Boulevard and was living in North Sacramento. His son, Walter J., had his own store on J Street. Walter was born in North Dakota in 1917, and a 1948 article in *The Sacramento Bee* indicates that his family arrived in Sacramento in 1920. The article describes the "pressure brake bleeder" that he invented while working in the hydraulic department of the U.S. Air Force in England during World War II. The war department awarded Walter a special merit citation in 1945 for his invention (Glackin *Sacramento Bee*).

Because Sacramento was the state capital with the potential for growth and because it had a reputation for being friendly and having nice weather, many Syrian-Lebanese were attracted to the area from the colder climes where they had first settled—on the East Coast, several mid-western states, and North Dakota. The 1939-40 directory lists over 75 families and the 1948-50 edition lists over 115.

Land was cheap in the outlying communities of Robla, Rio Linda, North Sacramento, and Wilton, so some families established farms in those areas. Others peddled dry goods and perishables, or worked for the Pacific Railroad, the Blue Diamond Growers (an almond factory), or local canneries. Eventually many opened their own businesses.

The extensive Kassis family of Sacramento followed this pattern. During the first decade of the 20th century, the George and Regina Kassis family of Zahle, Lebanon emigrated to North Dakota to take advantage of free land offered there. Everyone set about exploring different ways to earn a living to support the families they were in various stages of starting.

For example, Charles started as a peddler and later ran a general merchandise store in Rugby, N.D. Eventually he and his wife, Sophie, moved their family to Rio Linda. The family operated a chicken farm and opened the Chick-In Restaurant in town near Broadway and South Land Park Drive. They raised four children in Sacramento—Genevieve, Mike, Olga, and Lillian. (See page 45 for more about Mike Kassis.)

Assad Kassis and his wife, Maggie, also from Lebanon, were married in 1908. They farmed and operated a mercantile business in North Dakota. In 1919 they moved to Rio Linda and also were in the poultry business until 1928 when they opened the first of a chain of Stop & Shop markets at 28th and Y streets (now 28th and Broadway), where another grocery chain store stands today. They sold such items as ice, sacked coal, wood blocks, fresh fruits, vegetables, and canned food, and went on to open another 11 stores. Four of their sons—Frank, Lewis, Edward J., and Walter—operated the business after Assad passed away in 1945 and until the chain, later called Big K Markets, went out of business. Their fifth son, John, became a Sacramento physician.

Eli Kassis was only a teenager when he arrived in North Dakota. When he married Elizabeth Zinnie in 1921, they made their home in Williston, N.D. Eli owned a confectionery and homemade candy store, as well as an ice cream manufacturing business. He was the first to ship his own ice cream, as well as Eskimo Pie ® bars (originally called "I-Scream-Bars") hundreds of miles away—as far away as Montana.

The depression and dust storms ruined his business. Eli and Elizabeth moved to Sacramento in 1936 with their seven children—William, Dorothy, Harry, Gloria, Donald, Jeannine, and Carole. Philip, their eighth child, was born in Sacramento. William, Harry, and Donald served in the U.S. Air Force during World War II. All of the children married and produced a total of 36 grandchildren for George and Regina, the original émigrés. Harry became a doctor after graduating from Marquette University and Stanford.

The other members of the George and Regina Kassis family were Abraham and his wife, Freda; John and his wife, Eva; and Anna and her husband, John Shikany. Today numerous other grandchildren and great-grandchildren live in the Sacramento area and other parts of the state and country. Occupations among the various family members have included doctor, lawyer, engineer, ordained priest, teacher, real estate developer, retail outlet operator, movie theater manager, and newspaper owner.

Teenager Fred Naify arrived in Sacramento around 1914 with his two older brothers, Michael and James. The two brothers originally were in the linen importing business that they started in Atlantic City, New Jersey, when they

54

Naify Family in Damascus, Syria 1911
L-R: Sargius, Lee, Michael, George, Fred, Wadia
Center: Sarah & Mrs. M. A. Naify (Jim is absent.)

emigrated from Syria, but by 1916 had entered the movie exhibition business—first operating the Capitol Theater on K Street, but later acquiring T. & D., Jr. Enterprises, moving to San Francisco, and expanding their theater-ownership throughout northern California. (See pages 45, 48, 82, 91, and 95 for more about the Naify family.)

Fred retained his bachelorhood until he was forty, so he was free to move around managing his brothers' theaters. He was managing the Senator Theater in Chico when he entered into an arranged marriage with Marie Almaz. She was the niece of Rose and James Naify (Fred's brother) of San Francisco. She came to San Francisco in 1937 for an extended visit with her aunt and uncle, and by 1939 she and Fred were married and began their new life together in Chico.

All three of Fred and Marie's children, Jane, Jim, and John, were born in Chico, but the family moved to Sacramento in 1946 when Fred became a district manager for T. & D., and later United Artists Theaters. The Sacramento location was central to his district that stretched from Dunsmuir to Stockton, and also allowed the family to be closer to all of their relatives in San Francisco. Fred went on to found Naify Enterprises, which acquired a number of theaters in Sacramento, including the Rio Theater on J Street, featuring only Mexican films; the J Street Cinema on the current site of the Sacramento Convention Center, and several drive-in theaters in North Highlands, as well as one on Folsom Boulevard and the still existing Sunrise Drive In Theatre on Greenback Lane in Fair Oaks. His company also was involved in residential development, including a neighborhood of houses built on Naify Lane in northeast Sacramento near Del Paso Country Club.

Fred Naify - circa 1920s

Marie Almaz Naify was from Damascus, as well, and as a teenager in Damascus, she taught French and Arabic to younger students in a Roman Catholic Convent. The money she earned helped support her family. Marie is remembered by family and friends for the "delicious, homemade Arabic food" she required any visitor to the Naify home to eat.

Fred and Marie's children became successful in their own right. Jane is a vocational education teacher who helps people with disabilities return to gainful employment, as well as the former Secretary of the California Grand Jurors Association. Jim is an adjunct professor of Philosophy at Sacramento City College, and an expert on Middle Eastern philosophy. John, before his unexpected death in 1998, managed the J Street Cinema and owned and operated the Orpheum, a restaurant that featured his own stained glass art he created as a hobby. He was also an antique car collector and an avid fisherman.

Between the three children, they produced seven grandchildren for Fred and Marie. Fred died in 1981 and Marie in 1999. The rest of the family and several great grandchildren remain in Sacramento today.

(Family history and photographs courtesy of Jane Naify.)

As early as 1939, there were a number of Davids in Sacramento. Death records indicate that several of the Davids were born in North Dakota, so this must have been where yet another early Sacramento family first settled in America.

Alex David owned David's Market on Del Paso Boulevard; Ed David worked for the *San Francisco Chronicle*; Dr. Thomas H. David was a chiropractor on J Street; and Jimmy David owned a typewriter repair shop. Subsequently, Jimmy expanded his business to include an office supply store. David's Office Equipment Co. remains in operation on L Street today.

Fred David arrived in Sacramento in 1922 and in 1939 owned a cafe on 12th Street. By 1948 he had established the David Candy Company on Sixth Street. This wholesale tobacco and candy business is still in operation today on R Street.

Fred is most well-known for keeping the Sacramento Solons, a former Pacific Coast League baseball team, from leaving town in 1954. The Solons would eventually disband and move to Hawaii in 1960, with a brief return between 1974 and 1976, but the fans certainly were given a wonderful Christmas present in 1954. Fred and the Solons vice-president and general manager, Charles Graham, saved the day at the very last minute by pooling their stock holdings and keeping the Solons from being transferred to Vancouver, British Columbia in Canada (Conlin *Sacramento Union*).

According to the 1939-40 Syrian-Lebanese directory, the Sady brothers were operating the Sady Bros. grocery located on J Street; by 1948-50 they had moved the store to 28th Street. George Sady owned a poultry market at 16th and C streets until his retirement in 1947. His 1963 obituary in the *Sacramento Union* noted that before opening his market he had been a crew chief at McClellan Air Force Base in Sacramento.

Other Sady families lived in Sacramento during this period of time and death records show that all of the Sadys sojourned in Wisconsin before coming to Sacramento. Today a number of Sady families remain in the area.

Najeeb Salamy was one of two brothers in a family of six children, who emigrated from the village of Mar-Jayoun, Lebanon to the United States through Ellis Island around 1915. He had no job or money and did not speak English, but he was looking for the widely reported opportunities in America.

Jim, as Najeeb came to be known, promptly joined the U.S. Army and ended up as a combat soldier in Germany during World War I. Upon his return from the war, he entered the wholesale grocery business with his brother, Saad, and settled in Amarillo, Texas. The business did well for several years during and after the Great Depression of the 1930s.

In 1924 Jim had married Anna Elkouri, whose family came from the same village in Lebanon. In 1943, in the midst of World War II and tough financial times, the Salamys, with their two sons, Farris and Phil, moved to Sacramento where Jim opened Salamy's Market on J Street.

Until Jim retired in 1960, the little corner grocery was a proverbial "Mom and Pop" store—an all-day, seven days a week-operation, with no hired help. Both sons worked in the store after school, wanting to do all they could for their family. Through long hours of hard work, no vacations, and frugal living, Jim and Anna managed to put Farris and Phil through college, and Farris through Boalt Hall, the University of California, Berkeley, law school.

Farris became well-known in the Sacramento legal community, starting out his 37-year law career in the county in 1955 as a deputy district attorney. In 1959 he switched to the County Public Defender's Office, serving first as a deputy, then as the assistant public defender, and finally as the Public Defender for his last four years prior to retirement.

He defended such infamous murderers as "Vampire Killer" Richard Trenton Chase, Robert Nicolaus, and Aaron Mitchell. Chase was convicted of committing multiple murders and drinking his victims' blood; Nicolaus was convicted twice for killing family members 21 years apart; and Mitchell was convicted of killing a policeman, for which he was executed at San Quentin in 1967 (Mattson *Sacramento Bee*; Slater *Sacramento Bee*). Farris served also as President of the California Public Defenders Association.

The Salamy's other son, Phil, earned his degree in Business in 1959 from Sacramento State—today's California State University, Sacramento. Most of Phil's professional career was with the State of California, as a manager in the Real Estate Division of the Department of General Services.

Both Farris and Phil keep in touch with several of the Salamy family members who live in the family home in Mar-Jayoun, and are also still in the process of meeting other first cousins in Amman, Jordan. Farris and Phil continue to reside in the Sacramento area, as do their children and grandchildren.

(Family history courtesy of Phil Salamy.)

Joseph Mohamed was born in West Virginia, but his immigrant family moved to Sacramento when he was an infant. As an adult, he established Joseph Mohamed Enterprises, a land development company. Joseph created Mohamed Plaza and other developments in the Elk Grove area. He gave the streets of his residential developments Arabic names like Omar, Muhammad, and Ahmed (Al-Qazzaz, Amer and Doche *Arab Community*).

Over 50 other Syrian-Lebanese families were listed as living and working in Sacramento as early as 1939-40. They included Joe Bohamra, who owned a restaurant on Stockton Boulevard; Steve George, who was a sports editor for the *Sacramento Union*; the Joseph and Khoury families, Aziz Leishia, who owned a gas station; Charles and Ned Nabhan, who operated a barbershop on Del Paso Boulevard; George Saloman, who owned a market on Franklin Boulevard; and Tom Yasbek, who owned a linen shop on K Street. By 1948 the shop had become Yasbek's Children's Shop at the same location. Ernest Syufy, an uncle of Raymond Syufy who founded Century Theatres, (See page 97.) owned the Popular Shop on K Street.

Dr. Maurice Bisharat was one of the first Arab American psychiatrists in the area. In 1982 he and his wife, Mary, were founding members of the Sacramento Association of Arab Americans, formerly called the Arab-American Club of Sacramento. Maurice, also an accomplished landscape painter, passed away in 1998; Mary remains a leader in the Arab-American community. Their daughter, Katherine Bisharat, M.D., of Carmichael, took after her father in many respects, including having artistic talent.

In 2001 the Sacramento Association of Arab Americans reported that approximately 8,000 Arab Americans, some five generations-strong, were living in the Sacramento area. There are six Eastern-rite sect Christian churches, ten Islamic centers or mosques, and at least six Middle Eastern restaurants in the area—Cafe Morocco, Casablanca Moroccan Restaurant, Famous Kabob, Maaloufs Taste of Lebanon, Marrakech Morroccan (sic) Restaurant, and Shandiz Restaurant.

Many of the newcomers are professionals from the Bay Area who have come for affordable housing or the high-tech boomlet in the Sacramento region. For example, Kais Menoufy is the founder, President and CEO of Delegata, an e-business, system integration and technology consultancy.

Kais is from Egypt and completed undergraduate and graduate studies in Cairo. He then attended Harvard Business School in Boston.

In 1985 Kais moved to the San Francisco Bay Area as Vice President of TERA Corp. He acquired TERA in 1987 and founded SKAKS Technology. Before  starting Delegata in Sacramento in 2000, he was the Managing Director of International Operations for Indus International, Inc. in San Francisco. Kais has received several national and international awards for his business and technology achievements and is a recognized executive in the infor-mation management and high tech industry.

Kais Menoufy

Anton (Tony) and Iham Saca were both raised as conservative Catholics in Bethlehem; they married near the site of the manger where Jesus was born. The couple came to Sacramento to attend college. Following graduation they both obtained jobs with the State of California and began their family of two sons, John and David, and a daughter, Diana (Curley 69).

Tony Saca and the late Ghazi (Jessie) Karadsheh opened the first discount appliance store in Sacramento in 1973. Today Tony and several business partners own a chain of electronics and appliance stores—Filco Discount Centers—throughout Northern California and Reno, Nevada. Tony also invests in real estate and has developed a number of shopping centers and office buildings in Sacramento.

Tony and Iham have long been known in Sacramento for their philanthropy. Since 1993 they have been holding an annual benefit ball to raise money for Sacramento Food Bank Services.

Dr. Ayad Al-Qazzaz is a California State University, Sacramento professor who specializes in the Politics and

Societies of the Middle East. Born in Baghdad, Iraq, Ayad came to the United States in 1963 to obtain a Ph.D. in Sociology at the University of California, Berkeley.

Ayad has authored several books and over 40 journal articles on the Middle East. He frequently interviews with the media on current events related to the Middle East, and hosts a weekly local cable television program, "Focus on the Middle East." He lectures at conferences held throughout the world and has served on the boards of various Arab American organizations throughout the country. Currently he is the President of the Arab American Chamber of Commerce of Sacramento and the President of the Middle East Cultural Association of California State University, Sacramento.

Dr. Metwalli B. Amer and his wife, Rosalie Cuneo Amer, a third generation Californian, held professional positions they loved at two different universities in Cairo, but following Egypt's defeat in the 1967 Six-Day War, their outlook on life in Egypt changed. In 1969 Metwalli accepted an associate professorship at California State University, Sacramento, in the College of Business Administration. They settled in Sacramento in order to be near Rosalie's farming family in San Joaquin County.

Pleased to learn that there was a mosque in the downtown area, the family immediately became involved in the Muslim community. In 1987, seeing the need for a Muslim organization that transcended ethnic boundaries, Metwalli founded the Sacramento Area League of Associated Muslims (SALAM) and became its Executive

Dr. Metwalli B. Amer

Director. SALAM's primary focus is to provide Islamic education for Muslims and non-Muslims alike.

Following his retirement from CSUS in 2002, Metwalli continues his involvements with SALAM as well as with the Interfaith Service Bureau where he has been active for years and served as its president. In February 2003, SALAM expanded its management structure with a nine-member Board of Trustees. Metwalli was elected the first Chairman. SALAM recently opened its new Community Center. (See photograph on page 12.) Metwalli is also the President of the Council of Sacramento Valley Islamic Organizations, including ten mosques in Sacramento, Folsom, and Davis.

Professor Rosalie Cuneo Amer, with degrees in Library Science and History (Islamic Studies), has been a librarian at Cosumnes River College since the college opened in 1970. She has developed and taught Islamic humanities curriculum at the college, as well as Islamic and Arab culture curriculum in the Department of Humanities and Religious Studies at California State University, Sacramento.

Three generations of the Lebanese Joe G. Maloof family have resided in New Mexico since 1892. Joe operated a general store and raised his family in the northern part of the state.

Two of his grandsons, Joe and Gavin Maloof, are newcomers to Sacramento, but they already are well-known since they are the president and vice chairman, respectively, of the Maloof Companies. Among the Maloof family's portfolio of businesses is majority ownership of the Sacramento Kings National Basketball Association fran-

Joe and Gavin Maloof

chise—an annual playoff participant and the pride of "most" of Northern California.

Maloof Sports and Entertainment, a holding company, is also majority owner of the Sacramento Monarchs Women's NBA franchise, the Sacramento Knights World Indoor Soccer League franchise, and the 17,300-seat Arco Arena in Sacramento, as well as many other businesses in Las Vegas and New Mexico. Joe and Gavin's late father, George Maloof, was primarily responsible for expanding the family's business holdings before he died in 1980.

The Maloofs provide pleasure for millions of Kings', Monarchs', and Knights' fans, but they also assist countless community service groups and schools through their vast array of charitable projects.

The two brothers own homes near Arco Arena where they live most of the year. Their sister, Adrienne, lives in Sacramento also and is the secretary/treasurer of the Maloof company.

Their brother, George, Jr., is an executive vice president and heads the hotel division in Las Vegas, and Phil Maloof is an executive vice president and a former New Mexico state senator. Their mother, Colleen Maloof, serves as Chair of the Board of Directors of the Maloof Companies ("Maloofs Have Built a Business." *Arab-American Business*; Maloof Sports and Entertainment website).

CHAPTER NINE

San Joaquin Valley Arab Americans

THE SAN JOAQUIN VALLEY runs north to south for 300 miles between San Joaquin and Kern counties. Prior to the 1870s this portion of California had been a mixture of desert, grassland, and freshwater marshland, inhabited primarily by Native Americans and wildlife of all kinds. Stockton had been established during the Gold Rush, but Fresno and Modesto were the first extant towns to be established after that—during the development of a railroad line through the valley. Other towns followed when additional railroad lines were completed. During the same period of time the world-renowned agriculture was born with the development of gravity irrigation[44] and flood control measures.

Syrian-Lebanese farmers were among the first to transform the valley from desert land into one of the most productive farming areas of the state. The earliest arrivals settled in Reedley, Orange Cove, and Dinuba, having discovered these towns while peddling and making contacts in the area. Some purchased land and began farming; others opened small businesses throughout the San Joaquin Valley.

The 1939-40 Syrian-Lebanese directory lists over 35 families living and doing business in Stockton—many related families residing next door to one another or at least on the same street. By 1948 there were over 100 families.

[44] Water is delivered to the field by ditches, canals, or pipelines and distributed by gravity down the field.

Among these early residents were several market owners—C. M. Abdallah, Thomas Barakatt, Sarkis J. Barkett, Thomas Jacobs, and Tony Peter. Nemee and A. Abdallah owned a wholesale paper company, and Thomas M. Aboud owned the Aboud Mercantile Co. Peter and Josephine Francis owned a cafe and creamery. Other members of the Barkett family owned the Colony Club on Sutter Street and a liquor store on El Dorado Street. Joe Mattar owned a liquor store on Lafayette Street.

The Michael families owned a beauty parlor on Weber Avenue and Wilson Way called Michael's as early as 1939, as well as Michael's Department Store at the same address, and Michael's Market on South California Street. Wadie Michael had a grocery store on Grant Street.

The Rishwains, some of whom today are doctors and lawyers, had their start in Stockton in the grocery business— Tony Rishwain & Son wholesale grocers and the S. J. Rishwain grocery store on Weber Avenue. There also was a Rishwain Market on West Lane Street and a Rishwain Grocery on Cherokee Lane.

Other Stockton residents included Mrs. Anthony Badway and Michael Badway, John Habeeb, Mike, Harvey, and John Hakeem; a number of Jacobs, Tom Joseph, Charles and Joe Ossot, and Mrs. Julia Cruse, who operated the Cruse Inn on Wilson Way with the assistance of Carrie Hakeem.

Subsequent generations of these families remain in the Stockton area today and some are doctors, dentists, lawyers, university professors, restaurant owners, real estate developers, and large-scale farmers. A Superior Court judge, mayor, and city attorney descended from three of these families and several descendants are active in the community, serving on various boards and associations and providing financial support to charitable organizations.

The matriarch of the Zeiter family (first name unknown) arrived from Northern Lebanon in 1898 while the Spanish-American War was in progress. Her intent was to peddle small goods in order to earn money to support the five children she left at home. When she had earned and saved enough money to cover travel costs, she sent for her children.

All but one of the children remained in Stockton where they raised their own families. One son (name unknown) aspired to become a poet and realized that the United States was not the best place for him to pursue that dream. Just before the Depression swept the country, he returned to Lebanon where he became a recognized writer. In 1931 he was highly honored to be selected to deliver the funeral oration for the Arab world's greatest poet, Kahlil Gibran.

This son also fathered seven children with his wife. In 1948 the family moved to Venezuela to join family and work. One son, Henry, graduated from high school at the age of 16 and his father sent him to Assumption College in Windsor, Ontario in Canada, where other relatives lived.

Henry gained a passion for the philosophy and writings of St. Thomas Aquinas, but his poet father was quick to point out that he needed to pursue a practical career. So in his last year of college, Henry transferred to Western Ontario University where he could continue on in medical school. He graduated from the Western Ontario University Medical School at the young age of 23 and did his residency in ophthalmology in Detroit, Michigan at the Kresge Eye Institute.

Henry met his wife, Carol, at a hospital where she was a nurse pursuing her master's degree in pediatric nursing education. Carol had grown up in Detroit and she and Henry started their own family of two sons and two daughters there. In 1962 the couple relocated to Stockton, where many of Henry's aunts and uncles and cousins were still living, and Henry became Stockton's first ophthalmologist.

Henry founded the Zeiter Eye Clinic where his innovations in cataract surgery made him one of the nation's foremost eye surgeons. Henry has shared his techniques in clinical training throughout the world, including the Far East, Bulgaria, and his native Lebanon, where he collaborated with the medical society and the American University of Beirut to set up a surgical demonstration project.

Henry's nephew, Joseph, joined him in the eye clinic practice in 1980, and in 1985 the two doctors established a Surgicenter at the Zeiter Eye Clinic to eliminate the need to perform surgeries in nearby hospitals. In 1988 Henry's son, John, joined the practice as an ophthalmologist.

Henry and Carol, both now retired, have been active in the Stockton community, supporting the symphony, the Stockton Chorale and Chamber Music group, establishing a Homeless Shelter, and directing a foundation that provides scholarships for needy students.

Henry also serves on the Board of Governors of Thomas Aquinas College in Santa Paula in Ventura County. Henry and Carol's two daughters, Suzie and Camille, both attended the college. Their other son, Phil, is an architect in Grass Valley in Nevada County (Thomas Aquinas College Quarterly Newsletter).

There were a few Syrian-Lebanese listed in the 1939-40 and 1948-50 directories for cities in Stanislaus, Merced, and Madera counties. The Bashier Aweeka and Pete Francis families lived in Turlock;[45] Pete owned a cafe and gas station.

---

[45] There is a large population of Assyrians from the Arab country of Iraq, as well as from Turkey and Iran, living in Turlock and other nearby communities. However, because even the ones from Iraq do not consider themselves to be Arabs, they will be discussed separately in *California: An International Community – Understanding Our Diversity*.

There were two households of Andrews and the Paul G. Marks family in Delhi. Nagel and Ed Nahas lived in Merced; Ed was a rancher. By 1948-50, C. M. D. Najjar had joined the Nahas' in Merced.

George S. and Mitchell Santiago[46] operated Santiago's Store in Los Banos. In Madera, as early as 1939-40, Mike Khoury was a barber and there were two Syrian-Lebanese ranchers—William Moses and Joseph Basila. Joseph was growing grapes and cotton. By 1948-50 Nick Elias and Mike Koury resided in Madera, as well. Mike was a barber. Descendants of a few of these families remain in the area today.

Fresno County had a sizeable population of Syrian-Lebanese listed in both directories. As already noted, Reedley and Orange Cove were two of the first locations where they settled in the San Joaquin Valley. The 1939-40 directory listed 54 families in Reedley and 16 in Orange Cove; the 1948-50 directory listed 77 and 18, respectively.

The following is excerpted from *Reedley – A Study of Ethnic Heritage* compiled by the Reedley Historical Society in 1998. It describes some of the early families in Reedley and Orange Cove:

> The Joseph LaWand family arrived in 1903. Joe was a brick maker by trade, but had an ice cream shop in Oakland. His wife, Martha, was concerned about the earthquakes and convinced her husband, after the birth of their first son, George, to move to Reedley. Mr. LaWand worked for Craycroft Brickyard until he bought 20 acres on Manning Avenue. Many new settlers stayed with the LaWands and other families until they found a permanent home. There were three sons: George, a mechanic and machinist; Farris, a heavy equipment

[46]Mitchell Santiago may have been the son of Shaheen Santiago who was operating a general merchandise store in Fort Bidwell around 1940.

mechanic, truck driver and land leveler; and Sam, who worked the family farm and started well drilling with the Belknap family.

Mr. George, another early arrival to the Reedley area, sailed from Lebanon as a young man, traveling 'around the Horn' to arrive in San Francisco. He met and married his wife in San Francisco, and his first son, George, was born there. Later, the family tired of the Bay Area and moved to Reedley. George George opened his first grocery store on the corner of Dinuba and Alta in 1946. He moved to his present location at C and 11th streets in 1962, the former home of Ayoub Market. He continues to operate the grocery store known as George's Market.

Ambitious George Allen peddled clothes and utensils by packing them into suitcases and walking from ranch to ranch, spending the night at his last stop of the day. He later bought a Model T Ford, and covered much of northern California and over to San Luis Obispo selling his wares. A cousin, Anton Allen, operated a dry goods store on G Street next to the current Reedley Flower Shop.

In the late 1920s or early 1930s, Habib Grawan, with his sons, Walt, George,[47] and Willie, opened the Sun King Dairy (an ice cream parlor and candy shop) on 11th Street. Sun King later became a place where people gathered for coffee and conversation.

Other early businessmen included Charles Shaheen, who opened a grocery store in Orange Cove; Peter Paul, who operated a service station and grocery store at Alta and Manning avenues; Mike Baruti who opened a service station across the street; George Daher who had a grocery store on G Street in Reedley, and his cousin, John Daher, who farmed; Abraham Mussey, a dry goods merchant in Orange Cove; Tony Kady and Joe Mahwood who operated grocery stores; Joe Nicholas, a farmer and well digger; Saba Brother Trucking; and the Jadoon brothers, who were tavern keepers.

Other early Reedley residents were Alex and Charles Albert, Harry and William Khouri, John Shamoon, and

---

[47] The last section, entitled "People of Today", of Chapter XI *The Lebanese* of the Reedley Historical Society publication notes that Walt "The Fireworks King" and George Grawan were famous for the annual July 4th fireworks shows in Reedley.

M. Zerour. Another grocery store owner in Reedley was Sam Ayoub on 11th Street, until George George moved his store to this location in 1962.

Two Reedley farming families have been highly successful. Dan Gerawan is the current president of the family-owned company, Gerawan Farming, Inc., one of the largest tree fruit growers in the world. Founded in 1938 by his father, Michael, the company grows, packs, and markets peaches, plums, nectarines, and grapes on several thousand acres and employs several thousand workers. Gerawan Farming has been the leading force behind many regulatory reforms and improvements in farm worker conditions. (Adapted from Dan Gerawan's 1999 testimony before the Committee on the Judiciary of the U.S. House of Representatives.)

In 1949, Larry Shehadey purchased a major interest in Producers Dairy Foods, one of the few remaining locally-owned independent dairies in California—headquartered in Fresno. He became General Manager in 1951 and was the moving force behind the company's decision to build its own herd and dairy farms to ensure outstanding quality fresh milk. (Adapted from company website.)

Other early Orange Cove residents included Frank Beiknap, George Ellis, and Elias and John Jaffer. Descendants of many of these families remain in the area today.

Abdo Ali Ahmed was an example of a Yemeni who arrived in the 1960s to work as a farm laborer. Through hard work and a frugal lifestyle, he became a U.S. citizen and was able to open his own store in East Reedley—Ahmed's. Unfortunately, the 51-year-old father of eight fell victim to a suspected, but still unsolved hate crime shooting at his convenience store in October 2001. No money or merchandise was stolen; following the tragic event on the east coast on September 11, 2001, he had received threats.

The town of Fresno also had residents listed in the 1939-40 and 1948-50 directories—20 and 25, respectively. Included were James Baida, who had a photography studio; Benham Haddad, John Kassis, Abraham and Charles Sayeg, a rancher; Sam Thomas, a grocer; and Leon and George Zulfa. The Zulfas had a grocery market, as well as the Leon Zulfa & Son wholesale stand at the Central California Growers Market on El Dorado Street.

Habib and Ajiba Homsy emigrated from Aleppo, Syria to New York in 1898 with their two children, Anthony (6) and Marie (3). Other children followed: Julia in 1899, George in 1901, James in 1904, John in 1907, and Joseph in 1909. Habib was a merchant who exported and imported dry goods and oriental carpets.

In 1907, Habib bought two ranches in the Clovis/Fresno area, one for his own family and one for his brother's family. His brother's family ended up staying in Brooklyn, but the Habib Homsy family moved to Fresno. They lived near downtown and operated the two farms by themselves.

After completing high school, the Homsy's fourth child, George, attended the University of California at Berkeley—graduating with honors in civil engineering. He worked as a draftsman in the City of Fresno's Public Works Department for awhile, but then moved to the Bay Area to begin work on the George A. Posey Tube— the estuary tube that connects Oakland to Alameda. His professional career was cut short when his father passed away in 1923.

Homsy Family circa 1916
Standing on stairs L-R: Anthony, Ajiba and Habib
Boys on bikes L-R: George, Joseph, James and John

72

Homsy Family at the Ranch circa 1916
(1916 Hupmobile)

Homsy Family circa 1920
(1918 Marmon touring car)

George and Adele Homsy
Easter 1953

In 1988 George Homsy wrote a 21-page paper entitled "This is Your Life George Edward Homsy Sr." that recounts his family's history. One thing that becomes evident is the Homsy family's love of cars.

Homsys at George's May 1923
UC Berkeley Graduation
L-R: Agiba, Habib, James, Joseph, John & George
(1921 Essex Terraplane)

George & Adele Homsy Children
Easter 1953
J. Dennis, Barbara, George M.,
and Robert

George returned home to assist his mother in running the farms.

George bought the Clovis ranch from his mother and continued in farming—grapes and cotton—until the late 1960s when he sold the property to developers. Many of the newly created streets were named after the original farmers in that part of town, including Homsy Avenue.

George also kept busy throughout the years holding various positions in the agricultural industry, including service on the State Farm Debt Adjustment Commission, being appointed by Governor James Rolph, Jr. in 1937. He also did some bookkeeping and was the advertising manager for the *Central California Register*, a Catholic weekly newspaper.

In 1934 George had married Adele Slayman, the child of Lebanese immigrant parents. They raised their four children, J. Dennis, Barbara, George M. (Bud), and Robert, in the Catholic community centered around St. John's Cathedral and enrolled them in Catholic schools.

Dennis is the owner of a chain of stores—California Backyard and Nevada Backyard—specializing in outdoor furniture and accessories. He has three children, Stuart and Brian Homsy and Denise Homsy Tapken.

Barbara is a retired school administrator. She has four children, Kathryn Luthin Myers, Chris, Theodore, and Melinda Luthin.

George is a Stanford University Professor Emeritus of Chemical Engineering and a current professor of Mechanical and Environmental Engineering at the University of California, Santa Barbara. He has two sons, George and Robert Homsy.

The fourth Homsy child, Robert, is a research chemical engineer at Lawrence Livermore Laboratory. He has one daughter, Sarah.

Adele's side of the family has an interesting immigrant story of its own. Yuseph Slayman emigrated from Zahle, Lebanon around 1900. He was a peddler and, in 1905, acquired a 300-acre homestead in North Dakota. During his travels he visited a store in Pittsburgh, Pennsylvania run by the Andrews brothers. It was here that he met his future bride, Jemilli. Even though they were from the same town in Lebanon, they had never met before.

After their marriage in 1910, Yuseph and Jemilli moved to the homestead in North Dakota where Mitchell was born in 1911. The winters proved to be so severe that the young family surrendered the homestead to a brother and moved to Cambridge, Ohio, where Adele was born in 1913, and her siblings, Isabel, in 1915 and Victor in 1919.

In 1924 the family moved to Fresno where Yuseph joined his brothers-in-law working the fruit packing and farming business. Eventually Yuseph acquired his own growing and packing plant in Lindsay, which shipped fruit all over the United States. He became the largest shipper of pomegranates in the country.

Upon his death, Adele's brothers took over the family business. Adele's mother, affectionately known to all as "Aunt Jenny," was very active and influential in the Arab-American community in Los Angeles and the Greek Orthodox Church.

Adele's brother, Victor Slayman, is still living and resides in Porterville. Mitchell's son, Dwight, continues as a major shipper and exporter of pomegranates. George and Adele Homsy still reside in Fresno where, in 2003, they celebrated their 102nd and 90th birthdays, respectively.

(Family history and photographs courtesy of the George Homsy family.)

Finally, in the Fresno County cities of Fowler, Sanger, and Selma, nine Syrian-Lebanese families were listed in the 1939-40 Syrian directory, but only four in 1948-50. They included Lewis Mafawd, who was a restaurant owner; A. Daher, S. Shadid, and Nick Thomas. The latter three were ranchers. The Daher and Thomas families have remained in the area.

In Tulare County, both Syrian-Lebanese directories listed J. G. and N. G. Belliat in Dinuba, and Elias Mattar, Joseph Romonas, and Nick Thomas in Visalia. It does not appear that the Belliat, Mattar, or Romonas families remain in the area; there are many Thomases in Visalia, but they may or may not be Arab Americans.

As early as 1939-40, William Nabhan was the manager of the Hyde Theater in Visalia, as well as a movie theater in Lindsay. In the 1948-50 directory, Elias Mattar was associated with the Hyde Theater; perhaps he succeeded William.

Charles Andrews, a fruit packer; Ahmad Sharif (spelled Sheriff in the 1948-50 directory), a rancher; and Mrs. J. Slayman also worked and resided in Lindsay, where Slayman Fruit Co. was located. (See page 74 for more on the Slayman family.)

A few Andrews, who may or may not be Arab American, remain in Lindsay, but descendants from the other early families appear to have moved to other areas of the state, mainly the Bay Area and Southern California. Some Sheriffs live in neighboring Kern County, and as noted above, Victor Slayman lives in Porterville and Adele Slayman Homsy lives in Fresno.

There was a string of events between 1898 and 1904 that attracted newcomers to Kern County from everywhere. The Santa Fe Railroad arrived in Bakersfield in 1898, the Kern River Oilfield was discovered in 1899, the first oil pipeline was constructed in Kern in 1901, and by 1904 the Kern River Oilfield was the greatest producing area in all of California.

In Delano, at least by 1939-40, Mike Ellis owned a Standard Oil service station and Richard Sawaya operated a department store. Aref Orfalea opened a Malouf Mode O'Day store (See page 107.) on Main Street in Delano in the late 1940s. After his World War II paratrooper service in France and Belgium, he settled in the Los Angeles area where he was the vice president of California Fashion Creators, a garment manufacturing business that closed in 1978. Aref's son, Gregory, born in Los Angeles, is a renowned journalist, editor, poet, and author of several books, including *Before the Flames: A Quest for the History of Arab-Americans* that was a useful resource for this book.

Approximately 20 Syrian-Lebanese families lived in Bakersfield as early as 1939-40 and by 1948-50 there were 30 families, including Charles Bryan, Akel Hashim, who had a grocery store on East 18th Street; Charles Hashim, who had a dress shop on Baker Street; two other Hashims—Joe and Joseph; H. Lewy, who operated a market on Flower Street; Najeeb Malouf, who had a grocery on Edison Highway; William Romley, who was a projectionist at a movie theater; and Daas Simon, who was a grocer on Alta Vista Drive. Descendants of all of these families remain in Bakersfield today.

George and LaBiba Malouf emigrated from Lebanon around 1912. They originally settled in St. George, Utah, where George was in the produce shipping business. The Maloufs had five children, Linda—born in Lebanon; Albert, Theodore, and twins, Robert and Herbert.

In 1920 the family moved to Bakersfield, joining other family members already there. George continued in the produce shipping business and LaBiba was in the women's clothing business.

LaBiba loved to cook Lebanese food and taught her grandchildren some of her special skills. Gail Malouf, who today is in the real estate business in Bakersfield, was among those grandchildren fortunate enough to be exposed to this rich part of her family heritage.

In 1927 LaBiba became a member of The Order of Eastern Star in Taft, and in the 1940s, she transferred her membership to Bakersfield. She was also a matron of the Kern County Sheriff's Department at one time. One of her sons, Albert—Gail's father—was a Shriner and a Mason.

The Malouf families in Bakersfield had close relatives living elsewhere—mostly in the San Francisco Bay Area and Los Angeles. Many of them were in the clothing business, including the Maloufs who owned Mode O'Day. (See page 107.)

Another longtime family in Bakersfield is the Saba family. As early as 1939-40, George Saba had a dry goods store on Baker Street and Mike Saba ran Saba's Mens Wear down the street. The latter store remains in operation today.

There were a number of Haddad families in Bakersfield in the early days. Mary Haddad operated a beverage store on 22nd Street called Haddad Bros. Some Haddads were farmers and probably were related to Amean Haddad of Los Angeles—once known as "the Potato King of California." His company, Haddad Brothers Farms, grew potatoes in Bakersfield. (See page 104.)

A later Haddad to arrive in Bakersfield, and no relation to the early arrivals, was Elias W. Haddad, who came to the United States as a student from Lebanon. He arrived in California in 1955.

Today Elias owns six new car dealerships in Bakersfield. He enthusiastically adapted to California's way of life and remains appreciative of the many opportunities America has provided him.

Although the Central Valley was somewhat of an attraction for Syrian-Lebanese in the first half of the 20th century, it seems to have lost its allure as a destination for today's Arab

Americans. There are Islamic centers or mosques in Lodi, Stockton, Modesto, Merced, Madera, Fresno, Visalia, and Bakersfield, but these exist primarily for other Muslim ethnic groups. Although there are many Catholic churches in the valley, none appear to be Eastern-rite Christian churches. There are at least two Middle Eastern restaurants in the Central Valley, the Middle Eastern Restaurant in Fresno and the Cafe Med restaurant in Bakersfield, which serves Mediterranean and California cuisine.

Arab American Media

- Arabs began publishing newspapers in New York City in both Arabic and English, or a combination of both, as early as the late 19th century.
- Many publications have come and gone due to limited resources and readership, but one, *Al-Hoda* (*The Guidance*), has been in continual publication in New York since 1898.
- Today there are over 25 Arab-American newspapers and magazines, both print and on the Internet, published throughout the country, including several in California.
- *The News Circle Arab-American Affairs* magazine was founded in Los Angeles in 1972, and others published in California include the *Beirut Times Newspaper* and two magazines, *Al Jadid* and *Arab-American Business*.
- Arab-American television and radio programs are also available. The ANA Television Network broadcasts Arab-American programs via cable and satellite dish throughout North America. Arab programming is available on some local cable television stations. The Arab Radio and Television Network, a pay television station, provides Arabic family programming and entertainment worldwide.
- Radio programming in California includes Arabic Christian broadcasts that may be heard from San Francisco to San Diego on K E R I - AM 1180 radio station located in Bakersfield, as well as KHIS - 800 AM and KKLA - 1190 AM at selected times.
- Arab American media help Arab Americans keep in touch with their homeland and with one another, thus preserving their heritage.
- There are also American Muslim publications that serve the same purpose for Muslims of all ethnic groups.

Prejudice Towards Arab Americans

- Initially, the Arab ethnic group fared much better in America than other immigrant groups. Small groups were scattered throughout the country and they attracted little attention, assimilated quickly, and just went about their business—many becoming highly successful and influential members of their communities. If they were criticized at all, it was because others were envious of the fact that they were so financially successful.
- Arabs even escaped the ethnic slurs made about most other immigrants—until the 1920s when epithets like "horse breeder," "camel jockey," "black" or "dirty Syrian," and "Turk" began being used.
- However, after the June 1967 Arab-Israeli War,[48] anti-Arab sentiment worsened, and deepened further after the Arab oil embargo and the quadrupling of world oil prices that followed in the wake of the October 1973 Arab-Israeli War, the fall of the Shah of Iran in 1979, and the Gulf War of 1991. During the Gulf War, in addition to being called "camel jockeys," Arabs were called "Maddas lovers"—Saddam Hussein's first name spelled backwards. Other derogatory names have included "desert niggers," "sand niggers," and "greasy Lebs."
- There was a marked increase in hate crimes against Arabs and Muslims during the mid-1980s and another peak following the attacks of September 11th.
- Popular culture, particularly in America, has perpetuated the negative images of Arabs in movies, TV cartoons, comic books, and computer games. Rather than portraying them as normal people who work and have families, Arabs are singled out to play the role of villain, terrorist, belly dancer, harem girl, or desert dweller. The depiction of the latter as a characteristic of the Arab world is incorrect, since nomadic people, known as Bedouins, make up only about two percent of Arab people. Most actually live in urban areas.
- Other misconceptions about Arabs include:
  - "Anyone who became wealthy from oil is a 'sheik' and all sheiks have oil money." Neither is correct. A sheik can be the head of a village or tribe, a learned man, especially a theologian, or anyone who has memorized the Qur'an.
  - "Most Arabs are rich from oil." In fact, some are, but most are not. The area around the Persian Gulf[49] is one of the largest oil-producing areas in the world, but not all Arab countries produce oil.
  - "All Arabs are Muslims." Most are, but many are Christians of various denominations.
  (Adapted from Wingfield and Karaman ADC website; Shaheen 10)

[48] American support for Israel resulted in the castigation of Arab Americans.
[49] The sea that separates Kuwait and the other Arab Gulf states from Iran in the north is most properly known as the Persian Gulf. However, especially since the Iran-Iraq War (1979-90), many Arabs resent this name and prefer to call it the Arabian Gulf. The U.S. State Department calls it the Persian Gulf, but many diplomats feel it is safer to refer to the sea, as well as the region, as "the Gulf."

CHAPTER TEN

San Francisco Bay Area Arab Americans

IN THE LATE 19th/EARLY 20th centuries, Sonoma County attracted several utopian colonies, but it has never been a draw for Arab immigrants. The 1939-40 and 1948-50 Syrian-Lebanese directories listed only a few families, including the Bujazans and Alfred Cory, who worked at Safeway.

Abraham (Abe) and Nazara (Marcia) Maloof ran the ice

cream parlor in Guerneville around 1915, but after World War I, they closed the parlor, moved to Santa Rosa, and opened a bakery on Third Street.

Their son, Milton, served in the Army

Maloof's Ice Cream Parlor in Guerneville circa 1915
Photograph courtesy - Sonoma County Historical Society

Air Corps in World War II and was awarded numerous medals. He worked for 31 years at the Mare Island Naval Shipyard as an electrician. He lived to be 81 ("Milton Maloof" obituary).

Interior of Maloof's Parlor circa 1915
Photograph courtesy - Sonoma County Historical Society

Another son of the Maloof's, Fred, also worked at Mare Island and retired in 1959 as a painter (Zahn letter to author).

Fifie Malouf, of the George and Teckla Malouf family of Redondo Beach, lived in Santa Rosa at least as early as 1906 when the San Francisco earthquake occurred. She was good friends with the Abe Maloof family described above.

Fifie married her first of three husbands in Santa Rosa around 1907—R. A. Glenn, a confectioner of French candy. Around 1910 she married Jack Montgomery, another confectioner from Mexico City, and they moved to Los Angeles, where they established Fifie's Fresno Raisin and Nut Candy Company with outlets across the country.

Fifie Malouf - Photo courtesy of Willard F. Zahn, M.D.

Fifie divorced Montgomery in 1913, returned to Abe Maloof's Santa Rosa estate, and in 1919 married Willard Hoster, a local grocer. Fred Maloof was Willard's best man in the 1919 wedding.

Fifie and Willard built a public swimming pool and refreshment parlor in Santa Rosa, where Fifie gave swimming lessons and hosted weddings and other festive parties. In 1923, the couple moved to Redondo Beach (Zahn letter to author). (See page 114 for more about Fifie Malouf in Los Angeles.)

Michael Selby came to the United States from Beirut, Lebanon in 1902 and arrived in Santa Rosa in 1917. He became a barber at the age of 17 and continued cutting hair "off and on" until he was 92. Many of his customers were prominent residents of Santa Rosa. He operated

Michele's Cotati Inn with his second wife. The couple also had a dance studio in Santa Rosa. When Michael sold the inn, he returned to barbering full time. He also bought and sold real estate for 20 years. Michael has daughters and grandchildren who live in Eureka, Santa Rosa, and Middletown ("Michael Selby" obituary).

Wadia Khourie and Dr. Sargius Naify were part of the extensive Naify family involved in the movie exhibition business. (Also see pages 45, 48, 53, 91, and 95.) Wadia was widowed at a young age, so in the 1940s she and her four daughters were residing with her brother, Sargius and his wife, in Petaluma. In later years she lived in Sacramento with another brother, Lee.

Sargius had received his medical degree in Turkey and served as a physician in the Turkish Army. Unfortunately, upon arriving in America, he learned that he would never be able to practice medicine here because he had not received his medical training in English. He was not only the family expert, but advised most of the Arab American community in medically related matters—sort of the resident medical advisor (Naify interview).

Today there is a Middle Eastern restaurant in Santa Rosa—the East West Restaurant, but there are no Eastern-rite sect Christian churches or Islamic centers or mosques noted anywhere in Sonoma County.

Marin County has a sparse Arab American population. Shafik N. Kotite was the only Marin County resident listed in the 1948-50 Syrian-Lebanese directory. He was living in Kentfield. There are no Eastern-rite sect Christian churches in Marin County, but there is an Islamic Center in Mill Valley. However, those who are involved in this center include many non-Arab Muslims. No Middle Eastern restaurants are noted in Marin County.

Since the 1860s, ships had been departing from Martinez to deliver grains and fruits and nuts harvested in Contra

Costa County to ports all over the world. The railroad came through in 1879 and ferries operated back and forth across the Carquinez Strait between Martinez and Benicia until the Benicia-Martinez Bridge opened in 1960. Also, Shell Oil Company opened its refinery in 1914 and began shipping its products world-wide.

Therefore, it is not surprising that a couple of Syrian-Lebanese immigrants made their way to Vallejo, Benicia, and Martinez in the early days. In the 1948-50 issue of the Syrian-Lebanese directory, the Ferris M. Hajjar and William Syufy families were listed as living or working in Vallejo. (Also see page 84 and 97.) T. Freige was barbering in Vallejo, and Elias M. Jeha was managing the State Theater in Benicia.

Anthony, Isabelle, and Jean Saba were operating Saba's, a fashion shop for men and women on Main Street in Martinez, at least as early as 1934, when an advertisement in *The Contra Costa Gazette* advertised formals for $6.95, "every wash" dresses for $1, men's broadcloth shirts for 79 cents, and men's checked wool pants for $2.50.

Edward Ackel was the manager of the State Theater in Martinez in the 1940s. His wife, Essie, owned a fancy linen shop on Main Street. She sold fine linens and handkerchiefs (Martinez Historical Society).

George Nano lived in Pittsburg. Several families, including the Eddie and Fred Albert families, Philip Nemis, and David A. Shaheen lived in Richmond.

Edward Aweeka, Andrew Shahwan, and Ed Romley were listed as living or working in Walnut Creek. Edward G. Romley was a prominent builder in the Walnut Creek area. The Romley Construction Co. built St. Paul's Episcopal Church, the Walnut Creek library, the Las Lomas High School Music Building, the Elks Lodge, and numerous other commercial buildings. Ed's father, George, was the son of Shded and Afefey Romley from Lebanon. (See page 85.)

There are several Eastern Orthodox churches, four Islamic centers, and at least one Middle Eastern restaurant in Contra Costa County—El Morocco in Pleasant Hill. These are typically indications of a significant Arab-American community.

In Alameda County, there was a sizeable community of Syrian-Lebanese making their living as small business owners in the early part of the 20th century. In 1940, Fahmie Chimes Market was operating on College Avenue in Berkeley; Emil Armelli was selling insurance; and William Syufy, the father of the founder of Century Theatres (See page 97.), had a general store on Bancroft Way. In 1948-50, the Fahmie family was operating Fahmie Bros., a liquor store on Solano Avenue. There were another dozen or so families in Albany and Berkeley.

Over 60 Syrian-Lebanese families were listed in the Oakland, Alameda, San Leandro, Hayward, and Fremont sections of the 1939-40 directory, and by 1948-50 another 70 families had arrived. Many of the families were related or came from the same villages in their homeland, so there was frequent socializing in their neighborhoods and churches (Romley interview). The list of residents included Charles and Nick Abood, El-Abd S'ood, and Nick F. Zane.

Gibran N. Sahati sold rugs; George Shaheen was a tailor; Nicola Aboud was a shoemaker; and Abraham Ganem had a fruit stand on Telegraph Avenue. There were a variety of small storefront businesses in Oakland, including Mrs. L. Abood's dress shop on East 14th Street, Merched Aboumrad's dress shop on San Pablo Avenue, Nick S. Nicola's Roselyn Dress Shop on Tenth Street, Mitry Ofeish's linen and baby shop, Eli Mamiye's Milo Linen Shop on Telegraph Avenue, George Allen's grocery market on 22nd Street, M. Coody & Son grocers on West 8th Street, and Nick Skaff's grocery store on Peralta Street.

William J. Nabhan owned Nabhan Bros. Investment Co. and Abid El Hameed Jawad owned H. A. Jawad Syrian Importing Co. on 13th Street. Helen George operated a rooming house on Myrtle Street. In San Leandro the T. Maloof family owned a general merchandise store.

Around 1915 Shded Romley worked as a barber and shoe repairman in a rented storefront in West Oakland. In 1913, with $100 in their possession, Shded and Afefey Romley had immigrated to New York from Baskinta, Lebanon in search of a better life. They soon made their way west to California, with their first stop in Weed in Siskiyou County, where Shded worked in a lumber mill. An industrial accident, in which Shded lost his thumb, prompted the Romleys to move to Oakland with their children, George and Rose. They soon saved enough money from the barbering and shoe repair business to open their own grocery market at 7th and Campbell streets, eventually buying the building.

In the meantime, three more children joined the family—Mary, Tony, and James. The family lived behind the store with five people sleeping in one bedroom. Everyone worked hard and put in long hours; the end result was the development of a very successful business.

At the end of the work day, the Romleys always took time to enjoy the company of other families from their homeland— playing cards and visiting. Their church played an integral part in their lives. Shded's widowed mother joined the family for a time in 1936, but she soon returned to Lebanon, homesick for her former village.

The three boys followed their father into the grocery store business and later opened five more Romleys' Markets—two in Hayward and one each in San Lorenzo, Castro Valley, Concord, and Dublin. The Dublin store was the last to close in 1982. The brothers also spent ten years in the jam and jelly business (Romley interview).

Today a sizeable Arab American population remains in Alameda County. There are several Eastern Orthodox churches, including Melkite churches in Oakland and Fremont; five Islamic centers, and several Middle Eastern restaurants, including La Mediterranee and Papa's Restaurant in Berkeley, and Habibi Restaurant in Fremont.

In 1950 there were less than 20 Syrian-Lebanese families in the Silicon Valley. There were several branches of the Kirkish family in Sunnyvale and Cupertino. Abdellah Kirkish had a dry goods store on Murphy Avenue in Sunnyvale, and Charles Kirkish was a dentist. John Sayig had a grocery on El Camino Real in Sunnyvale. B. Ganem, Mrs. Thomas Johns, and Joe Samaha resided in San Jose, and the D.G. Teeny family lived in Campbell.

But these small numbers would soon change as Arab Americans became key players in the Silicon Valley's rise to prominence in the high-tech industry. Through their ownership of, or employment with technology, real estate, law, and financial firms they have helped build the infrastructure of the area.

There is a particularly large concentration of Arab Americans in San Jose. While most arrived from overseas during the last 50 years, many also moved from San Francisco in search of a more suburban lifestyle.

There are several Orthodox parishes in the South Bay Area, including a Maronite church in Millbrae, a Melkite church in San Jose, and Byzantine churches in Los Gatos and Mountain View; there are five Islamic centers. At least three Middle Eastern restaurants are located in the South Bay—Zeeba's Kabob House and Shalizaar Restaurant in San Mateo, as well as Ali Baba in South San Francisco.

Braham and Raheja Aboud arrived in Sunnyvale in 1917 via Williston, North Dakota. (In America, Braham used the English "Abraham" and Raheja went by "Jennie.") Abraham had come to the United States with his mother and siblings from Machgara, Lebanon in 1900 to take advantage of the government land grants available in North Dakota. Jennie, a cousin, joined the family in North Dakota later. She was the only person in her immediate family to leave Lebanon.

When Abraham was 30 and still unmarried, his mother, Nesta, encouraged Abraham and Jennie to marry, which they did. As a married couple, they applied for a homestead in Williston. They established a farm on the land that still belongs to members of the Aboud family today.

The Aboud's first child, Sadie, was born in 1907, followed by Rose in 1909, George in 1910, Josephine in 1913, Edna in 1915, and Helen in 1917. Farming was a new occupation for the Aboud family; in Lebanon they had been tanners. After ten years of harsh winters and failed crops, the family moved to Sunnyvale, following two of Abraham's brothers who had already moved to the Bay Area.

In their new home in California, four more children were added to the family: Michael in 1920, Fred in 1922, Lucille in 1924, and Victoria in 1926. At one time or another, everyone in the family worked in the neighboring orchards. Abraham contracted to pick all the fruit from an orchard employing his family. He also worked at Stanford University as a gardener until he reached retire-

Aboud Family - Back row L-R:
Edna, Rose, George, Fred, Michael, Helen, Josephine, Sadie
Front row L-R: Lucille, Jennie, Abraham, Victoria

ment age. Jennie worked in the canneries, as did her children when old enough, and when they were not in school.

(Aboud family history and photographs courtesy of Winnie Kingsbury and Peter Fatooh.)

San Francisco's Mediterranean-like climate had been attracting Syrian-Lebanese families to the city even before the turn of the 20th century. After the 1906 earthquake and fire a large number of Syrian-Lebanese living in New York, Detroit, and Canada came to the city responding to reports about the reconstruction and provisions needed.

Four generations of the Joseph and Takla Farrah family of Barti, Lebanon have resided in the San Francisco Bay Area since shortly after the 1906 earthquake. Nicholas J. Farrah was the first to leave the family's tobacco farm to come to America in search of better economic opportunities. He worked in Pennsylvania coal mines for two years before setting out for San Francisco. Out of a horse-drawn wagon, he sold dry goods to the rural farmers and ranchers south of the city. In 1914 he purchased a small dry goods store on Mission Street and ten years later replaced it with the N. J. Farrah Department Store that he constructed on a lot in the same block. In 1928 Nicholas opened Farrah's Shoes down the street.

L-R: Joseph, Edward, George, Julia & Michael Farrah at George & Julia's Golden Wedding Anniversary 1978

Between 1914 and 1920, Nicholas was busy helping his three brothers and widowed mother immigrate to San Francisco. One brother, Michael, was killed on the job in an industrial accident, but the other two brothers joined Nicholas in the retail business. Sam opened his own clothing store, S. Farrah, in the same neighborhood, and

George worked in the department store. All three brothers married and two of the families had a total of four children between them. The Nicholas and George Farrah families lived in adjacent flats above the N. J. Farrah Department Store. (George's 92-year-old wife, Julia, still resides there.)

George purchased Farrah's Shoes from his brother in 1939 and opened a second shoe store in 1948 to provide jobs for two of his three sons, Joseph and Edward. The two sons had to leave their father short-handed for two years while serving their country in the Korean War, but soon Joseph became the manager and later owner of the shoe stores. Edward became the manager and later a partner of the department store, which his parents purchased from Nicholas in 1955 when Nicholas and his wife, Elizabeth, retired and moved to Los Angeles. Edward later went into a parochial school uniform manufacturing business with his brother-in-law and in 1989 converted the Farrah Department Store into Farrah's Uniform Center. A second retail parochial school uniform store was opened in Burlingame in 1992.

Michael, George and Julia's third son, broke the family mold and became an attorney after graduating from the University of San Francisco School of Law. All three of George and Julia's sons married and bore nine children, eight of whom reached adulthood, three of whom continue to reside in San Francisco. All of the retail stores have since either been liquidated or sold.

(Farrah family history and photograph courtesy of Joseph A. Farrah.)

The Kaleel and Maryanna Fatooh family arrived in San Francisco in 1934 in search of a better life than what they had found in Canada. In 1901, 20-year-old Kaleel emigrated from Batroun, Lebanon, to establish himself in Nova Scotia, Canada, before sending for Maryanna and his infant child, Maude. Maryanna's mother was living in

San Francisco, but Kaleel chose to immigrate to Canada because a friend in Nova Scotia sent him the money for his passage. Eighteen-year-old Maryanna arrived with Maude in 1902.

In Lebanon, Maryanna's father trained Kaleel to be a

barber, but in Nova Scotia he worked as a peddler, traveling throughout the neighboring countryside. In time he and Maryanna were able to purchase a general store in Florence, Nova Scotia. They moved their family, which now included six more children, into the living quarters on the second floor.

Education was very important to the Fatooh family. They needed Maude to help out at home and in the store, but each

Back L-R: Charles and Maryanna
Center: Fatooh Fatooh (Charles' father) of the other children—
Front L-R: Michael, John, and Maude Michael, John, Wilfred, Florence, Negla, and Abraham—as soon as they turned five, were sent to a French boarding school operated by nuns a fair distance from their home.

In 1924 the Fatooh's store caught fire and the entire building, including their home on the second floor, burnt to the ground. Maryanna told Kaleel she was ready to move to California. Upon their arrival in San Francisco, Kaleel opened a grocery store on Chenery Street. In 1943 he sold his store and went to

Fatooh's store circa 1936

work in the shipyard. (Kaleel called himself Charles, but in San Francisco he was known as "Charlie.")

Five of the Fatooh children made the move to San Francisco with Kaleel and Maryanna. Maude married, but was widowed at a young age. She had one daughter and supported herself by operating a grocery store. Michael became a fireman. John graduated from the University of California, Berkeley, where he was on the swim team. He became a junior high school math and physical education teacher.

Wilfred was the last to emigrate from Canada, arriving in San Francisco in 1939. He worked as a railroad clerk until the outbreak of

Charles & Maryanna circa 1937

World War II, when he was given the choice of joining the Canadian or the U.S. Army. He chose the U.S. Army. After the war he returned to his railroad clerk job and studied to become a real estate broker. Wilfred married Helen Aboud of the Sunnyvale family described on page 86.

Florence stayed in Canada. Negla was a homemaker and Abraham was a house painter—both in San Francisco.

(Fatooh family history and photographs courtesy of Winnie Kingsbury and Peter Fatooh.)

The 1939-40 Syrian-Lebanese directory lists over 250 families and by 1948-50 another 30 families were living and working in San Francisco. Advertisements in both directories paint an interesting picture of who some of these families were and how they were making a living and enhancing life and commerce in the city.

The Naify family bought a number of ads in the San Francisco section. Michael Naify had a page advertising

T. & D., Jr. Enterprises, Inc.; Dr. and Mrs. Sargius Naify advertised the California Theater he managed in Petaluma; Mr. and Mrs. Fred A. Naify advertised the Senator Theater they managed in Chico; Mr. and Mrs. George A. Naify advertised the Victoria Theater they

Mrs. Naify's 90th Birthday Celebration in Redding 1941
Photograph courtesy of Jane Naify

operated on 16th and Mission streets; and Mr. and Mrs. Jim A. Naify reserved a complimentary page in their name, with their home address on Normandie Terrace. (See pages 45, 48, 53, 82, and 95 for more about the Naify family.)

Dr. Alexander A. Kirkish placed an ad for his dental practice. Joe and Al Droubie advertised their grocery and deli on Cole Street, and Mr. and Mrs. John Khouri advertised their grocery, meat, and vegetable store on 14th Street. Joseph Malouf Co. sold *Jody Slips*—touted in their advertisement to be "'Wearpruf' guaranteed slips."

Other businesses listed in the directory without advertisements also help paint a picture of the Syrian-Lebanese community in the mid-1900s. James Ackel had a cleaning and press shop; Kareem Azar and George Saba were barbers; Jack Waheed was a shoemaker; Ades Bros., Inc. was an import company; Howard Hajjar was a theater manager; Andrew McKenna owned the Nile Cafe on Turk Street, and William Almed ran a restaurant on O'Farrell Street; A. E. Anthony & Son was a dress manufacturing company; E. A.

Anthony sold sports wear; Joe M. Armelli owned Mayfair Liquors; Nick Sahatis owned Marlo Packing; Joseph Bradway had a print shop; N. E. Zeibak and Co. manufactured linens and Tom Hajjar sold them; and Fred Ayoob, Charles E. Anthony, George Fakhoury, Jack Haddad, Joe Kayrallah, John and Mike Khouri, S. G. Saadallah, Peter Totaha, and the Essaff Bros. were all in the grocery business in the city.

Dr. Carl Rayes was an optometrist, and Dr. N. J. Sadala was a dentist. Fred Salih was a contractor; Richard Cory was an electrical engineer; and Mike and N. P. Kafoury owned an electrical supply company.

Some of the other family names included Aboud, Ansara, Ayoub, Badran, Dudum, Habeeb, Haber, Hafiz, Jadallah, Jordan, Kazaka, Mallick, Murr, Nasser, Nicholas, Roditti, Romley, Syufy, Thomas, and Weygand.

Today there remains a very large population of Arab Americans in San Francisco. It is estimated that Arab Americans own approximately 300 corner stores in San Francisco, but they also make up a large portion of the professional workforce in the city—doctors, lawyers, college professors, and business executives leading a wide array of corporations. The Arab Cultural Center is located in San Francisco; there are a number of Eastern-rite churches in San Francisco, an Islamic Center in San Francisco, and over a dozen Middle Eastern restaurants in San Francisco and neighboring San Mateo County.

Much of the Bay Area had an influx of Palestinians between 1948 and 1967 when they were fleeing political persecution and seeking to improve their lives. In 1984 it was estimated that there were nearly 20,000 Palestinians, with almost 30 percent coming from Ramallah, a city near Jerusalem (Sifri 82). Today the Palestinian population is concentrated in the suburbs south of San Francisco.

Arab Americans in the Movie Industry

The **Abraham Nasser** family from Zahle, Lebanon, arrived in San Francisco in 1901. Abraham's brother, Albert, had been operating a confectionery business in the city since his arrival in 1894, but Abraham's family began peddling fruit in the South of Market neighborhood. Abraham and his wife, Emily, eventually had seven sons and one daughter, the oldest child being 17 in 1901. The children's names were William, Elias, Anne, Richard, George, Henry, James, and Ted, who was born in America in 1908.

In 1905 the family moved to Eureka Valley—today known as "the Castro"—and opened a fruit store near Albert's candy making business. Soon the Nasser family envisioned a new market for their candy: the popular nickelodeons that charged a mere five cents for admission to watch moving pictures. The Nasser Bros. Theatre chain was launched in 1908 with the opening of a nickelodeon called The Liberty. It was located on 18th Street. It was followed by another nickelodeon on Castro Street called the "Castro Street Theatre." That was followed in 1910 by a third theatre called "The Castro," that seated 400 people in what is now Cliff's Variety Store on Castro Street.

In 1922, the Nassers opened their most elaborate theater yet, called the "New Castro" just a few doors up the street from "The Castro." On the date it opened, the Nassers closed "The Castro." The new "Castro" (the word "New" was dropped shortly thereafter) had a strong Spanish

Courtesy of
Theatre Historical Society of America
Steve Levin Collection - 1948

influence with ornate Italian flair. It was the first movie palace designed by Timothy Pflueger, who was to become a famous architect. It seated 2000 people. The theater was designated an official city landmark in 1977.

Timothy Pflueger went on to design other movie palaces for the Nassers such as the Alhambra Theatre in San Francisco in 1926 and the Alameda Theatre in Alameda in 1932. Pflueger also designed extensive renovations for the Nassers' New Mission, Fillmore, and Royal theaters in San Francisco.

At the peak of their exhibition days, the Nasser family had 13 theaters in the San Francisco Bay Area. Their financial success in the early 1920s enabled the Nassers to build new homes in the exclusive St. Francis Wood residential neighborhood overlooking the Pacific Ocean.

In 1947, four of the Nasser brothers, George, Henry, James, and Ted broke into the Hollywood scene by purchasing General Service Studios, a nine-acre movie studio dating back to 1919. In 1951 the four brothers entered the television business by renting their studio production facilities to the producers of such TV shows as *I Love Lucy* (for its first two years), *Our Miss Brooks*, *The Lone Ranger*, and *Burns & Allen*. They also produced several movies at the studio before selling it in 1976.

Today the Nasser family still owns two movie theater buildings, The Castro, which they operate, and the Alhambra building, which has been converted into a health club that shows movies, leased by Gorilla Sports. Theodore Dennis Nasser, the son of Ted Nasser who is still alive at 95, currently is President of the family companies that own the Castro and Alhambra buildings.

(Family history courtesy of Theodore D. Nasser.)

Two brothers from Syria, **Michael** and **James Naify**, started out in Atlantic City, New Jersey in 1912 operating a linen importing business. They eventually moved their import business to California, settling first in Sacramento. However, following a trip to San Francisco in 1915 to exhibit at the Pan Pacific Exposition, they decided they were in the wrong business. Apparently their booth was across from a nickelodeon. Impressed with the numbers of people visiting the nickelodeon, Michael and James soon were in the business of operating their own nickelodeons and regular movie theaters, first in Sacramento and later in the San Francisco Bay area and throughout northern California. T. & D., Jr. Enterprises, acquired from the original operators of the chain, Turner and Duncan (thus the name T. and D.), was headquartered in San Francisco. Early theaters included luxurious art deco theaters like the Senator built in Chico in 1928, the State built in Oroville in 1928, the State built in Red Bluff in 1929, and the Cascade built in Redding in 1935. (See page 46.)

Michael's two sons, Marshall and Robert Allen, started in the movie business themselves as ushers and projectionists in their father's theaters. They went on to become owners of 50 percent of the United Artists Theater Circuit in 1950, until they sold their share in 1986. They also were early pioneers in the cable television industry in the 1950s.

In 1964 Marshall became the president of Magna Theatre Corporation, which produced the movie *Harlow* in 1965. Following Marshall's retirement and before his death in 2000, he served as co-chairman of the board of The Todd-AO Corporation.

The Naify brothers had other interests outside of the movie industry. In 1967, for example, Marshall, as president of UA Theater Circuit, and in partnership with the owner of the "The Hungry i Club" in San Francisco, opened a new, larger post-Bohemian version of the famous supper club.

Marshall owned and raced horses for many years, and in the 1990s he owned a thoroughbred breeding farm in Kentucky. Both brothers were perpetual members of the Forbes Four Hundred.

The Naifys have long been philanthropists, supporting such organizations as the Yerba Buena Center for the Arts in San Francisco.

Several of Michael and James' brothers also were involved in the theater business. Dr. Sargius Naify, the third brother in the family after Michael and James, managed the California Theater in Petaluma. (See page 82 for more details about Sargius.)

Fred, only 12 or 13 at the time, departed Ellis Island for Atlantic City, New Jersey with his two brothers. While his brothers were still operating their linen business and before they discovered that there was money to be made in the film industry, Fred was already working in the movie theater business—delivering movie reels on his bicycle to theaters throughout Atlantic City on a rotating basis—this before the advent of multiple film duplication processes. After the three Naify brothers moved to California, Fred became involved in theater management in his brothers' theater chain business and later established a diversified business of his own in Sacramento. (See pages 48 and 53 for more details about Fred and his family.)

Lee Naify, the fourth brother after Michael and James and the seventh of the eight Naify children, managed theaters throughout northern California—Petaluma, Martinez, Redding, Chico, Sacramento, Monterey, and Pacific Grove. He had his own theater in Los Angeles for a time before returning to Sacramento, where he died suddenly in 1959 at the age of 61. At the time of his death, he was managing his brother Fred's Rio Theater on J Street. He had no children and lived with his widowed sister, Wadia, from time to time.

Four brothers from the Lebanese Syufy family emigrated to America in the early 1900s. In 1941, one of the brother's sons, **Raymond J. Syufy**, at the young age of 23, opened his first movie house in Vallejo called The Rita. He proceeded to open other theaters, including many drive-in theaters, throughout northern California under the parent Syufy Enterprises company. Eventually he established the headquarters of Century Theatres in San Francisco to operate the circuit of theaters that today spans 11 states, with 75 theater locations and over 850 screens.

Raymond pioneered a new architectural design for movie theaters with the opening of his dome-shaped theaters, like the one built in Sacramento in 1967. The beamed, circular ceiling, along with a sloping seat arrangement and widescreen and stereophonic sound offered every theater-goer an equally first-class movie experience.

Two of Raymond's sons, Raymond, Jr. and Joseph, took over Century Theatres after their father's death in 1995.

Other Arab Americans Involved in the Film Industry

- **Nassour Studios, Inc.**, where over 100 independent films were shot under the William and Edward Nassour family's ownership from the 1940s to '80s, including *High Noon*, starring Gary Cooper. Several television programs were filmed there, including *Abbot & Costello* and *My Three Sons*. Today William's son, William Nassour II, is the studio director of DH1 Studios Inc., a diversified media and entertainment company in Beverly Hills and New York.
- **Mardi Rustam**, born in Kirkuk, Iraq, came to the United States in 1954. In the 1970s he became an actor and a movie producer, director,

and screenwriter while serving as the President of International Film Laboratory, Inc., Rustam Productions, and Rustam Investment Corporation.

- **Fouad Said,** from Cairo, Egypt, where he worked for MGM before moving to Los Angeles to attend the University of Southern California's School for Cinematography. He was the cinematographer for *Take the Money and Run*, the 1969 Woody Allen film, and producer of the 1972 *Across 110th Street*, starring Anthony Quinn. In 1964, while working on the TV series *I Spy*, he designed Cinemobile, the first customized van for filming on location.
- **Moustapha Akkad**, born in Aleppo, Syria, received his Masters in Cinema Studios at the University of Southern California. He is best known for producing the eight movies of the "Halloween" horror movie series. He also directed two movies about the Arab-Islamic world—the 1976 *The Prophet*, the 1977 *The Message*, and the 1981 *The Lion of the Desert*. His son, Malek, directed and produced *Psychic Murders*.
- Lebanese actor, **Michael Ansara**, who was married to Barbara Eden for several years, is best known for his Native American roles in the 1956 television series, *Broken Arrow,* and the 1959 western series, *Law of the Plainsman*. He currently does TV cartoon voiceover work.
- The late **Victor Tayback** was born to a Syrian-Lebanese family in Brooklyn. His family moved to California when he was in high school and he graduated from Burbank High. In the 1960s, after serving in the U.S. Navy, he began his television acting career in TV commercials and TV guest-star appearances. Eventually he became a regular on several series, including *Alice*, in which he played Mel.
- **Mario Kassar** was born in Lebanon in 1951. In 1969, at the age of 18, he created a foreign distribution company, Kassar Films International. In 1976, he formed Carolco Pictures, Inc. with Andrew Vanja, and the two went on to produce the *Rambo* series of action movies and other films. In 1989 Kassar became the sole chairman of Carolco; he was the executive producer on such films as *Terminator 2: Judgment Day* and *Stargate*. In 1998 Kassar and Vanjar teamed up once again and formed C-2 Pictures. They also produced, *I Spy* in 2002 and *Terminator 3: Rise of the Machines* in 2003.

CHAPTER ELEVEN

Central Coast Arab Americans

THE NORTH END of the Central Coast—Santa Cruz, Monterey, and San Luis Obispo counties—has never had many Arab Americans. The Syrian-Lebanese directories published in 1939-40 and 1948-50 list Dr. Joseph Samaha in Santa Cruz, Elmer Assad in Watsonville, Joseph Gabriel in Hollister, who owned the Hollister Ice Co.; Andrew Dovolis and Jerry Yazbek in Salinas, Nicola Afana in Paso Robles, and Mrs. William Keffury in Santa Margarita, who owned a service station there in 1948.

Some Gabriels, Dovolis', and Afanas, who may or may not be related, remain in the area today. There are a few Yazbaks in Ventura and El Dorado counties, who may or may not be related to the Jerry Yazbak family.

There were a few more Syrian-Lebanese families listed in the two directories as residents of Santa Barbara and Ventura counties; today there is a sizeable Arab American population here. Many probably have moved from Los Angeles in search of the more suburban lifestyle.

Both of the Syrian-Lebanese directories listed the Azar family as residents of Santa Barbara—Icer, Sam, and Saleem—at three different addresses. There was an Azar Market in Summerland, east of Santa Barbara.

A 1972 obituary for Kaisser Azar described him as the operator of several small grocery stores in Santa Barbara from 1919 through 1945. He was born in Yucatan province, Mexico, but grew up in Lebanon. He had relatives in Brazil, so this may have been one of the Syrian-Lebanese families that was rerouted to South America when attempting to immigrate to America. Several Azar families remain in Santa Barbara today.

Skip and Rose Shalhoob lived in Santa Barbara as early as 1939-40. A 1968 obituary for Napolean Shalhoob, Skip's brother, reports that they were the children of Lebanese parents, the Very Rev. Methodias J. Shalhoob and the former Anastasia Shwiery. The parents lived in Santa Barbara until their deaths in 1944 and 1967, respectively.

Napolean served in the U.S. Navy during World War II and practiced law at one time. He also was a businessman involved in mining, men's clothing, grocery retailing, and manufacturing. At the time of his death, he owned The Haberdasher store on State Street in Santa Barbara ("Shalhoob Rites" obituary). Today several Shalhoob families remain in Santa Barbara.

Katherine Koury's 1977 obituary described her as "one of Santa Barbara's more colorful residents." She was born in Syria in 1890 and immigrated to Texas in 1902 with her family, the Nicolas'. Katherine married John Koury, but was widowed in her late 20s. She moved to Santa Barbara with her two children, Mike and Olga, and in 1919 opened a grocery store—Koury's Market—on Santa Barbara Street. She not only sold groceries and meats, but also costume jewelry, dry goods, and clothes. The Kourys lived behind the store, which survived through two depressions, the 1925 earthquake, and chain store competition. Katherine put both of her children through school.

In 1959 Katherine was named for the Hats Off award by the Advertising and Merchandising Club. She was cited for her kindness and generosity and called 'the friend in need for all peoples.' She also was known for her "boldness" when confronting armed robbers on two separate occasions. Her brother, Sam Nicolas, also lived in Santa Barbara ("Koury services" obituary).

In 1939, Jim Ayub was selling insurance in Ventura and Mitchell Slayman owned a bowling alley, but he was not listed in the 1948-50 directory. Other Ventura County communities had a smattering of Syrian-Lebanese residents and business owners, including George Owen, who owned a dry goods store in Santa Paula; the Rihbanys, who were grocers in Fillmore and Santa Paula; and Miss Dalail Al Murr, who owned a dry goods store in Moorpark. In Oxnard, Charles and George Habib were grocers; Nicholas Murr owned Murr Ready To Wear; and Toofy Samaha owned a Pontiac agency.

Descendants of most of these early Syrian-Lebanese families remain in the area today. No Eastern-rite Christian churches are noted, but there is an Islamic Society of San Luis Obispo and an Islamic Center in Newbury Park, which may have Muslim Arab Americans who attend it. There are at least two Middle Eastern restaurants in Santa Barbara—Chef Karim's Moroccan Restaurant and Shalhoob's Specialty Deli.

Photograph courtesy of Jeff Marschner

The Statue of Liberty was a welcoming beacon to Arab immigrants arriving at Ellis Island.

Arab Organizations

- Unlike most other ethnic groups in America, the Arabs were slow to establish nationwide secular institutions. They were more focused on assimilating into American society and becoming successful members of their communities. Many changed their names, style of dress, and learned English.

- The introduction of the quota system of 1924 sparked some Arab Americans to become politically active and in the 1930s a federation of Syrian and Lebanese clubs was formed throughout the country. However, any concerns about cultural or social issues waned during World War II.

- With the creation of the State of Israel in 1948 and the 1967 War in Israel and Palestine, Arab Americans were galvanized to unify on a national level. The popular support in America for Israel resulted in Arab Americans being ridiculed.

- In an effort to educate Arab Americans, as well as the rest of America, the Association of Arab-American University Graduates was formed in 1967.

- This was followed in 1972 by the establishment of the first Arab-American lobbying organization—the National Association of Arab-Americans. Politicians tend to be reluctant to accept support from Arab-Americans because they fear the loss of the Jewish vote.

- In 1980, in response to an increase in discrimination and prejudice, the American-Arab Anti-Discrimination Committee was established.

- In 1985, the Arab American Institute was organized, to help Arabs to become involved in politics.

- Today, more and more Arab Americans desire to maintain their cultural identity, settle in cities where Arab American communities already exist, and have stronger ties with their country of origin.

- Various other secular Arab-American organizations exist throughout the country, including the National U.S.-Arab Chamber of Commerce, American Arab Chamber of Commerce, American Federation of Ramallah,[50] the Arab American Medical Association, local Arab-American student organizations, local Arab-American Republican and Democratic clubs, local Ramallah clubs, and local cultural centers.

- Christian Arab Americans have organizations, which include the American Lebanese League and the Lebanon Information and Research Center.

- A number of national and local religious organizations for Muslims exist that include Arab-American members—the Islamic Society, the Council on American Islamic Relations (CAIR), the American Muslim Council, the Muslim American Society, the Muslim Arab Youth Association, the American Druze Society, the Druze Council of North America, the Muslim Public Affairs Council, the Islamic Chamber of Commerce (ICC), and various Muslim professional societies. Following 9/11 Muslims of all nationalities made a concerted effort to become more involved in their communities in order to reach out to non-Muslims and calm their fears about Islam.

[50]Ramallah, located ten miles north of Jerusalem, was occupied by Israel after the Six-Day War in 1967.

CHAPTER TWELVE

Los Angeles County Arab Americans

LOS ANGELES has the largest concentration of Arab Americans. This has always been the case within the state and today it is true for the whole country, as well. Los Angeles, of course, is the second largest city in the United States.

When the railroad arrived in Los Angeles in 1876—connecting Los Angeles and San Francisco, finally Los Angeles began catching up with the San Francisco Bay Area that had developed so rapidly during the Gold Rush of the late 1840s and 1850s. Prior to 1876, Los Angeles had remained fairly isolated from the rest of the state and the country. Other events that precipitated development included the discovery of oil in 1892 in downtown Los Angeles; the development of San Pedro Harbor in 1907; the arrival of the first motion picture studio in 1908; the completion of an aqueduct to transport water from the Owens Valley in Inyo County in 1913; and the establishment of the aircraft industry in southern California during World War II.

A large population of Syrian-Lebanese was settled in Los Angeles County as early as the 1890s. The Syrian-Lebanese directories of 1939-40 and 1948-50 assist in determining where they were living and what types of businesses they were operating.

By 1940 approximately 25 families were living in the San Fernando Valley towns of Tarzana, Encino, Van Nuys, San Fernando, Burbank, and Glendale, and by 1950 those numbers had tripled. There were several doctors, lawyers, construction contractors, restaurateurs, manufacturers, and other small businessmen; a realtor, a teacher, and a rancher.

104

Family names included Abood, Boshae, Haddad, Malouf, Maloof, Mittrey, Nadar, Najjar, Nassour, Obegi, Sawaya, Sayeg, Shalhoub, Shamoon, Thomas, Waian, and Abdun-Nur.[51]

In 1906, A. S. Abdun-Nur, from Douma, Lebanon, entered Northwestern University Medical School in Illinois. After his residency in Colorado, he moved to Tarzana, where he became the only physician in the community. His son, John, and John's son have carried on the medical tradition in the family. John graduated from the School of Medicine of the University of Southern California in 1954 (Abdun-Nur questionnaire; USC website).

Amean Haddad from Zahle, Lebanon, owned Haddad Brothers Farms, one of the largest potato growers and wholesalers in the United States at one time. He assumed the title of "the Potato King of California" after the death, in 1926, of the former title-holder, George Shima, a Japanese potato farmer in the Stockton area.

Amean arrived in California in 1920 and worked as a butcher in Los Angeles before becoming a potato farmer with fields in four western states. In California, Haddad Brothers Farms were located in the San Joaquin Valley. Haddad's potatoes supplied Safeway stores with half of their stock. Amean was self-educated and active in his local community of Encino (Haiek *1984 Almanac*; Orfalea 295).

Naseeb Michael Saliba, also of the San Fernando Valley, was born into a Lebanese immigrant family in Ozark, Alabama. The Saliba family eventually settled in Los Angeles and Naseeb graduated from Los Angeles High School in 1932.

[51]In the 1960s and '70s the section of Hollywood east of the 101 Freeway was the leading point of arrival for Armenian immigrants and refugees from Iraq, Lebanon, Syria, Turkey, and Soviet Armenia. Armenian immigration to America will be examined in the chapter on Armenians in the forthcoming book, *California: An International Community*.

After graduation, Naseeb moved to Idaho to open an automobile dealership and garage. He sold the dealership and then began buying and selling service stations, subsequently moving back to Los Angeles.

Naseeb began his construction career in a management position with his uncle's construction firm, but formed his own firm in 1942—N. M. Saliba Company, which became one of the most successful heavy construction companies on the west coast, with operations in California, Nevada, Idaho, Arizona, and Utah.

At the young age of 42, Naseeb retired in order to spend more time with his family, but he remained involved in large public works projects through his bonding and consulting work. He helped many beginning contractors and engineers develop their own successful firms.

In 1970, Naseeb formed Tutor-Saliba Corporation, which became one of the largest privately held international general contracting firms in the world, with projects that included the San Diego Convention Center, Tom Bradley International Airport Terminal, the Los Angeles Metro Rail System, the San Francisco BART railway system, the San Francisco International Airport Terminal, and the Alameda Corridor project in Los Angeles. In 1996, Naseeb retired from Tutor-Saliba Corporation.

Naseeb has been the recipient of both professional and personal awards, the latter including the Ellis Island Medal of Honor in 1997 for his successful Lebanese business leadership, as well as accommodations from past presidents, governors, and other government officials. In addition, he has been recognized by world leaders throughout the Middle East for his accomplishments as an Arab American.

Naseeb is a board member of many organizations, including the Antiochian Orthodox Christian Archdiocese of North America. He also is Chairman of the Board of his son's construction and engineering firm, Saliba Corporation. (Adapted from Ellis Island Medal of Honors website.)

Twenty-five Syrian-Lebanese families were living in the San Gabriel Valley towns of Pasadena, San Marino, San Gabriel, El Monte, Azusa, Whittier, Monterey Park, and Montebello by 1940, and half of the families lived in Pasadena. After World War II many Arab Americans migrated to Los Angeles from the East Coast, lured by the post-war boom in the economy and the warm, dry weather. Early Syrian-Lebanese arrivals gravitated towards Pasadena and nearby towns. The numbers of families listed in the 1948-50 directory in the San Gabriel Valley increased to a total of 90, and some of these located in additional towns— Altadena, Monrovia, Alhambra, Rosemead, and Pomona.

There were several doctors and a lawyer; several manufacturing companies; a teacher; a number of grocery markets, including M. & G. Gantus Market in San Marino and Mary Tarbye's grocery on East Mississippi Drive in San Gabriel. George J. Abdelnour had a general merchandise store on Azusa Avenue in Azusa, and Nick Abdelnour's dry goods store was located next door. The children's wear manufacturing companies of Joe Butros and Hanna Bros. were established in El Monte. Other family names included Assad, Hanna, Koury, Mallouf, Malouf, Nahra, Nassief, Roum, Salhie, Sayeg, Shahayha, and Waian.

Today many Arab American doctors, lawyers, bankers, realtors, and construction firm owners live in the San Fernando and San Gabriel valleys. Most came during the third wave of immigration when Arab professionals were able to enter the United States under the terms of a professional-preference clause in the Immigration and Naturalization Act of 1965. (See page 35.)

Joseph Haiek, a Palestinian, emigrated with his wife and four children from Jerusalem in 1967; he became an American citizen five years later. Joseph is the publisher of *The News Circle Arab-American Affairs*, an Arab American magazine. In 1972 he founded The News Circle Publishing House in Glendale, which periodically publishes the *Arab-American Almanac*, a comprehensive reference book about the Arab-American community throughout the United States.

Many Arab Americans living in the San Fernando and San Gabriel valleys today commute to downtown Los Angeles to work in their professional workplaces or in the garment and other large-scale industries. In the earliest days of the City of Los Angeles' development as an industrial center, Syrian-Lebanese established companies to manufacture bed linens, lingerie, and women's apparel. One such company was Mode O'Day, originally called the Western Garment Manufacturing Company when established by three Malouf brothers—A. B. Malouf, W. B. Malouf, and B. B. Malouf.

The nationally known Mode O'Day was a women's garment manufacturing and sales firm that owned its 12-story headquarters building in downtown Los Angeles, another plant in Salt Lake City, and more than 300 retail outlets known as Mode O'Day stores in 20 states (Zeidner, Utah History website). The advertisement taken out in the 1939-40 Syrian-Lebanese directory described Mode O'Day's frocks as "famous all over the West – for style – quality – and workmanship – retailing at $1, $1.98, and $2.98."

With the huge numbers of Syrian-Lebanese living and working in the incorporated portion of Los Angeles when the 1939-40 and 1948-50 directories were published (over 1,200 families in 1940 and more than 1,600 in 1950), a better sense of who this large population was and how they were making a living and enhancing life and commerce in Los Angeles can be gained from reviewing some of the advertisements placed in the directories.

In the 1939-40 issue, a number of Los Angeles grocers purchased advertisements, including Elias Nassief; Kallel's Market—one owned by Albert Kallel and one by Widey Kallel; Mike Moses; Balian's Market, Inc.; Imported Groceries, owned by N. M. Haidar; and Hatem's Market, owned by Joseph Hatem.

George M. Ofiesh advertised his Angeles Wine & Liquor Co. and Ackel Shaheen advertised his beverage, tobacco, and candy store. Mrs. Agnes Joseph Tahan & Son advertised their Syrian Pastry & Confectionery store that specialized in baklawa, kunafee, and other sweets.

Barkett's Drive-In Market owned by Mike Barkett was a combination malt shop and cafe, grocery, meat, and beverage market located at West Sunset Boulevard and North Alvarado Street. A few restaurants advertised in the directory, including the Sultana Cafe, managed by William Neima and owned by Fred Neima; and Wadie's Cafe, owned by W. Shasheen.

Sawaya Bros. and Nasef Ellis sold wholesale dry goods. A. Nassour was president of Castilian Productions Corporation that sold household and Castilian granulated soap.

A. Shaheen & Brother sold rugs, tapestries, and bedspreads; Be-Hannessy, owned by Phares A. Be-Hannessy, sold distinctive furniture, rugs, draperies, and upholstery in Beverly Hills; and Joseph M. Armelli owned World Importers, Inc., with branches in San Francisco and Seattle.

Various clothing merchandisers advertised in the directories, including Mode O'Day, as noted above. George A. Nichols, a native of Tripoli, Syria, advertised his Nichols & Co.—a wholesaler of men's and boys furnishings and manufacturer of men's and boys sweaters. Advance Apparel Co. manufactured uniforms, slacks, suits, and children's wear. Ackary Lingerie Company placed an advertisement, as did Mrs. Joe Butros for her Helene's Fashion Shoppe.

Syrian-Lebanese were involved in the construction industry with George Mittry serving as a general contractor; Harper & Reynolds Corp. providing contractors' supplies and builders' hardware; E. K. Wood Lumber Co. providing lumber; and George M. Boosalis' Roofing & Tile Company offering stucco and interior painting services.

In the automotive business, Al E. Baker & Co. advertised that they had been selling used cars since 1924; Baida Bros. offered automotive service; and Elias Khoury and Arthur Mamey owned Ambassador Motor Sales.

In 1939-40, Joe Murr advertised his Morningside Recreation Center in Inglewood and the fact that he owned fourteen "20th Century Bowling Alleys." George D. Sphier advertised his law practice and Leon M. Saliba promoted his general insurance business. Finally, Our Ladies of Lebanon Church and St. Ann Church placed an advertisement.

In the 1948-50 issue of the Syrian-Lebanese directory a number of Los Angeles grocers purchased advertisements, including Najar Market owned by Thomas A. Najar and Charles Dowaliby; Jack Mobayed Meat Market on Telegraph Boulevard; the Riverside Market in North Hollywood, owned by Vic Damus and George Hamati; and two repeat advertisers, Elias Nassief and Barkett's Drive-In Market.

Sawaya Bros. advertised their wholesale dry goods business again. Mr. and Mrs. George Beebe advertised the art linen and distinct gifts they sold in Beverly Hills, and Z. N. Baida invited visitors to his Beverly-Wilshire Art Galleries.

Nichols & Co. advertised again in 1950, and were joined by Sunny-Cal Sportswear Co. managed by Edward T. Maloof; Jackie & Annette of California, manufacturers of children's and teenage sportswear; Tina of California, manufacturers of children's dresses and sportswear, and owned by M. J. Hanna, J. G. Butros, and William J. Hanna; S. Orfaleo & Co., which manufactured blouses that were the "Charm of

Hollywood;" Jr. Fashions of California, owned by Nick Ghiz; Najla Stephan & Son Edmond, which manufactured ladies' robes and lounge pajamas; Jabour Manufacturing Co., which manufactured children's wear; Holly Mode Inc., owned by Joe Murr, William Jabour, and Pete Murr, that made men's sports shirts; and Corey of California, owned by Adele Khoury and Andrew Abdo, which manufactured ladies' and children's wear.

Only one restaurant advertised in this directory—The Raffles on Degnan Boulevard, owned by Mitchell Boureston, who claimed they served "excellent food." Joe Murr advertised his Morningside Recreation Center again, and was joined by Magnolia Bowling Center, Inc., owned by Mrs. Sophia S. Mussellem and George J. Khair. William and Edward Nassour also ran an advertisement for their Nassour Studios Inc. on Sunset Boulevard in Hollywood. (See page 97 for more about Nassour Studios.)

Finally, a realtor and general insurance service provider, George A. M. Fuleihan; a real estate investor, Norman N. Mamey; the manager of the Paramount Citrus Association, Lewis Ghiz; two attorneys, Merton E. Albee and Albert W. Thomas; a physician, George E. Fakehany, M.D.; a tailor, C. K. Badran; and Al Baker, the used car dealer who advertised in 1939-40, all purchased advertisements in the 1948-50 directory.

Approximately 120 families were living in the West/Central Los Angeles towns of Pacific Palisades, Santa Monica, Venice, Inglewood, Watts, Culver City, and Palms by 1940, primarily in Venice, Inglewood, and Santa Monica, in that order. These numbers remained stable through 1950.

The directories of 1939-40 and 1948-50 list a number of grocers, including Charles E. Haddad, Hector P. Baida, and the Gabriel family in Santa Monica; Farris M. Solomon in Venice; and Balian's Market on South La Brea Avenue and Anses Joseph Market on Arbor Vitae Street in Inglewood. In Watts, James Lopez had a market on Compton Avenue; John Cora had one on East 113th Street; and Tom David was a wholesale grocer on Wilmington Avenue nearby.

E. K. Badran sold fruits in Palms, and Mrs. Abbdo Hilaiel had a beverage shop in Santa Monica. In Watts, George Gabaley operated a dry goods store on East 107th Street; Fred Tumb had one on East 103rd Street; and W. N. Sawaya owned a department store on East 103rd Street. Richard Nasser had an art goods store in Venice.

There were a number of Syrian-Lebanese restaurateurs in West/Central Los Angeles, including Bashara Haddad, Fred Kabbash, Leo Khoury, Nicholas Veluhaky, and Charles and Ruffie Hallal in Santa Monica; and Terry A. Mansur on the corner of Hawthorne Boulevard and the Imperial Highway in Inglewood. Phillip Kiralla operated a playhouse on Ocean Front Walk in Venice. Boureston's Billiard Parlor was located on the Imperial Highway in Inglewood, and Joe Murr owned a bowling alley on East Manchester Drive nearby.

Dr. Alex Mulki had his medical office on Grevillea Avenue in Inglewood, and Madelyn Boureston operated a beauty parlor on East Manchester not far away. Lloyd H. Hilaiel was a policeman in Santa Monica; William Shishims was a barber on Stanford Avenue in Venice; and A. Kiralla operated a garage on East 105th Street in Watts.

Elias Abdelnour owned apartments on Breeze Avenue in Venice. Munyer Bros., owned by Alex, Joseph, and Victor, was a contract builders firm in Inglewood.

Other residents in West/Central Los Angeles included M. R. Gabriel and Saleem Morakady in Culver City; A. M. Nicola in Palms; Hal Baida and Charles E. and Elias Haddad in Pacific Palisades; Michael and Nicholas Haddad in Santa Monica; Albert and Alexander Akoury; S. Haddad, and the

Khoury family in Venice; and Mrs. George Haddad, N. Scaff, and Henry Waian in Inglewood.

Finally, in the South Los Angeles/Long Beach area of Los Angeles County, approximately 75 families were living in the towns of Bell, Lynwood, Compton, Hawthorne, Hermosa Beach, Redondo Beach, Wilmington, San Pedro, and Long Beach in 1940, and another 35 families by 1950.

The Syrian-Lebanese directories of 1939-40 and 1948-50 list a number of grocers, including, in Hawthorne, Abdelnour & Hatem Market on North Hawthorne Boulevard, and Zarour Bettar Market on Felton Avenue; and in Bell, Ameen Gannam on Avalon Boulevard, and Albert Hamud on East Anaheim.

Azar & Azar Dry Goods was operating on East Orange Boulevard in Compton; Charles Azar owned an appliance store on Avalon Boulevard in Wilmington; and Bert T. Malouf owned a dress shop just down the street. Ed Barbari owned a furniture store on East Anaheim Street in Long Beach, and Jacob E. Hanania was a jeweler on Atlantic Avenue in Long Beach.

N. Skaff & J. Munyer operated the Centinela Cafe on South Hawthorne Boulevard in Hawthorne; and Joe Houraney had a cafe on South Long Beach Boulevard in Compton.

Several tailors, some presumably in the same family, were available for the residents of West/Central Los Angeles, including Ernest Coury in Hermosa Beach, Henry Coury on North Broadway in Redondo Beach, and William Coury & Son on Diamond Street in Redondo Beach. Ed Coury owned a cleaners on Torrance Boulevard in Redondo Beach. In Wilmington, Mrs. L. George owned a gas station on West Wilmington Avenue.

In Hawthorne, Wadie Shaheen ran a pool hall on North Hawthorne Boulevard, and George S. Allen owned a hotel on East Ocean Boulevard in Long Beach. Tom Simon was an artist in Hawthorne; George Afana had a print and design shop in Long Beach; and Jamel Afana had an art shop in Long Beach.

There were several professionals in the neighborhood— Thomas F. Doumani, Ph.D., residing in Wilmington; George and Wadieh S. Shibley, attorneys in Long Beach; Dr. John V. Malouf, a chiropractor and an attorney, with an office on Atlantic Avenue in Long Beach; and Dr. Malouf's sister and brother-in-law, chiropractors, as well, with their Zahn & Zahn office on East 7th Street in Long Beach. (See below for more about the Shibley and Malouf/ Zahn families.)

Finally, several Syrian-Lebanese families owned apartment buildings in the South Los Angeles/Long Beach area. Elias Azar owned an apartment building in San Pedro; F. G. Mosey owned the Fair Apartments in Long Beach; and the George Malouf family owned apartments on The Strand in Redondo Beach. (See below.)

George Shibley, one of the attorneys listed above, was born in New York in 1910, the son of a well-educated immigrant family from Lebanon. Both of his parents were graduates of the American University of Beirut and spoke perfect English. His uncle served as the Governor of Ellis Island for many years.

George's family moved to Long Beach in 1921, where his father worked as a pharmacist and his mother taught school. Following graduation from Stanford Law School in 1934, George established a criminal defense law practice in Long Beach. Following his death in 1989, George's wife, Eleanor, described him as the attorney who "took cases that no one else would." He was known in the legal community as a fighter for the underdog, taking such cases as *People v. Zammora*, which led to the unrest depicted in the movie "Zoot Suit Riots;"[52] and the early appeals of Sirhan Sirhan, the convicted murderer of Robert F. Kennedy ("Zoot Suit Riots." PBS website; Shibley questionnaire).

After their marriage in 1876 in Zahle, Syria, George Nasser Malouf and Teckla Malouf traveled to Australia and many other countries around the world. George was a professional candy maker, with a specialty people called his "Turkish Delight" confection. The Malouf's travel destinations were usually locations where a fair exposition was being held; they made and sold their candy at the fairs.

They arrived in the United States in 1890, with three daughters and one son, all born in Zahle. The family lived in Los Angeles for the first few years, where George and Teckla operated the Turkish and Egyptian Bazaar on South Spring Street that sold Syrian artifacts—clothing, utensils, handcrafts, and religious icons. Two of their daughters, Wadeaa and Fifie, and Teckla's sister, Zahdie, worked at the bazaar and lived in the Malouf home on New High Street, along with another relative, Daisy Malouf, a dressmaker. By 1897, according to the Los Angeles City Directory, the Malouf's bazaar had expanded to two locations, one on North Main and the other on South Brawley Street; the family lived on Alpine Street.

The Maloufs welcomed Angeline to the family in Los Angeles, and Martha in 1898, while in Seattle for a short time. By 1900 the family was living in Niagara Falls, New York, where John was born. (George and Teckla had six other children while still in Zahle, but they died in infancy.)

[52]*People v. Zammora* was the mass trial of 22 Mexican Americans indicted for the murder of another Mexican American. The successful appeal case was tried by another attorney, because George was drafted into the military immediately following the original trial. It affected constitutional law throughout the country by prohibiting mass trials. The appeal was successful due in part to the numerous objections George put on record during the trial. "Zoot Suit Riots" was a film about the racial tensions that led to the Los Angeles riots in the summer of 1943 following the original trial.

In Niagara Falls, George owned grocery stores and Teckla ran a rooming house for immigrant relatives and fellow countrymen from Zahle. Her accommodations were typical of the housing available through the Syrian networking system. (See page 29.) They also continued their travels to fair expositions while living in New York.

In 1920, tiring of the severe winters in Niagara Falls, the Maloufs returned to California. George and Teckla bought the Laurel Apartments on The Strand where Beryl Street meets the ocean in Redondo Beach. The apartments were promptly renamed The Malouf Apartments.

George was severely disabled with arthritis by this time, so Teckla kept busy taking care of George until his death in 1929, and managing the

Teckla Malouf & Wadeaa

apartment building until it was condemned in the 1950s (see below). Teckla also traveled with her daughter, Fifie, until she was bedridden herself from a stroke. She died in 1955 in Hermosa Beach.

George and Teckla's oldest daughter, Wadeaa, moved to Niagara Falls with them. In her late teens/early 20s she was a popular professional Syrian lecturer. She would appear attired in a beautiful native costume and spend over an hour describing the life and customs of Syria, all earning rave newspaper reviews.

Wadeaa Malouf in N.Y.

Her future husband, William Geary Zahn, an American from Pennsylvania with Bavarian roots, had met the Malouf family as early as 1894 at the San Francisco California Midwinter International Exhibition. He was an electrician by trade and routinely held supervisory electrician jobs at fair expositions. William and Wadeaa struck up a romance and were married at the Portland, Oregon, Lewis & Clark Centennial Exposition in 1905.

The couple started out their married life as confectioners in Niagara Falls, but later enrolled at the Palmer School of Chiropractic in Davenport, Iowa, earning their degrees in 1921. They moved to Long Beach and established the Zahn & Zahn chiropractic office in front of their residence on Seventh Street that remained in operation for 30 years. (Bonnie Zahn, D.C. keeps the family name on the homestead marquee today.)

In the meantime, William and Wadeaa produced seven children, only three of whom reached adulthood. Two sons, Dr. Malouf Zahn and Dr. Victor S. Zahn, became chiropractors like their parents, and later added law degrees, following the lead of Uncle John Victor Malouf. The youngest, Willard F. Zahn, M.D., practiced obstetrics and gynecology for 30 years. Willard is the only surviving child of this branch of the family, along with his children and grandchildren and those of his deceased siblings and one sister-in-law, Victor's widow, Esther Zahn, D.C. Since retirement, he has immersed himself in his family's genealogy; he generously provided the Malouf family history and photographs for this book.

When William Zahn passed away in 1943, Wadeaa, through careful and methodical planning, was able to eventually build the LACO Trailer Haven in Torrance, retire from her chiropractic practice at the age of 65, and live in a trailer and manage the park until her death in 1952.

George and Teckla's second daughter, Fifie, at the young age of 14, chose not to move with the rest of the family when they moved to Niagara Falls. She continued selling the family candy in California, but joined the family whenever they had a concession at a world exposition.

Fifie appeared with John Philip Sousa's band at the Paris Exposition of 1900. "During the playing of patriotic numbers, she posed with an American flag as the Goddess of Liberty" ("Old Phone Book" *Santa Rosa Press Democrat*). At the St. Louis Fair in 1904, Fifie reputedly invented a new way of eating ice cream using her husband's sugar waffles as "cones" when a nearby ice cream vendor ran out of plates. (See page 23.)

Fifie led a varied and colorful life. She followed in her father's footsteps and became a professional candy maker. She married three times, but never had any children. She lived in Santa Rosa for a time with her first husband, R. A. Glenn, a confectioner of French candy. In 1910 she married Jack Montgomery, another confectioner from Mexico City. They moved to Los Angeles, where they established Fifie's Fresno Raisin and Nut Candy Company with outlets across the country.

She married Willard Hoster in 1919 in Santa Rosa, (See page 81 about Fifie's life in Santa Rosa.) and in 1923, the couple moved to Redondo Beach, where they built the Mt. Lebanon Apartments across Beryl Street from her parents' Malouf Apartments. (Neither apart-ment building remains today because the first six blocks of The Strand were destroyed in the 1940s and '50s due to tidal changes caused by con-struction of a breakwater, as well as annual winter storms.

Malouf & Mt. Lebanon Apartments on The Strand, Redondo Beach - 1921

When the apartment buildings were finally condemned in 1953, Fifie and her mother, Teckla, moved to Hermosa Beach.)

During the 1920s and '30s, Fifie and Teckla often hosted social events for the Syrian community in the area, including the gatherings of the Ladies' St. Anne Altar Society of the Melkite Catholic Church, weddings, and various chiropractic association functions of Wadeaa's. The Malouf hospitality table was always loaded with "goodies." With the

arrival of company the covering sheet was removed with a flourish and the hospitable Arab greeting of "FUD-dal" (partake, enjoy, chow down). Food ranged from Near-Eastern delicacies to All-American wiener roasts, and the music from piano to Victrola and to the native Levantine versions of the lute and zither.

At some point after her father's death in 1929, Fifie opened the Happy Hour Cafe, which was attached to the north side of The Malouf Apartments. During World War II and the years of blackout, U.S. Coast Guardsmen assigned to The Strand and other lonely GIs were frequent patrons of her cafe. Her nephew, Willard Zahn, refers to Fifie as the "one-woman wartime USO."

She also was referred to as "Madame Fifie" (with no verifiable explanation, but several suggestions) and was known for her philanthropy and love of travel, gold mining, and piloting vintage airplanes. She rarely missed a Redondo Beach City Council meeting, flaunting her weakness for limousines and furs. Her grand life was celebrated by the Redondo Beach Historical Society on the 100th anniversary of her birth on February 14, 1986.

George and Teckla's other children were Dr. John Victor Malouf of Long Beach, also a chiropractor, and also a lawyer; Jubert G. Malouf, of Hollywood, Florida; and Virginia Tope of Grants Pass, Oregon. The two

Fifie Malouf Attired for Gold Mining 1939

other daughters, Angeline and Martha, died in the flu epidemic of 1919 while the family still lived in Niagara Falls.

(Family history and photographs courtesy of Willard F. Zahn, M.D.)

The Syrian-Lebanese have been attracted to Los Angeles ever since the first wave of immigration. That attraction has continued with more recent immigrants of all faiths and nationalities. Even inaccurate population figures attest to that, as do the existence of over 15 Eastern-rite sect Christian churches, over 30 Islamic centers or mosques (which may or may not serve Arab Americans), and over 20 Middle Eastern restaurants—all good indicators of a significant Arab American population in the area.

Well-Known Arab Americans
and Contributors to American Culture

Arab Americans have frequently appeared on the "Who's Who" list in America. There are too many to list here, but a few of the more familiar names are: George J. Mitchell, former U.S. Senator; John H. Sununu, former New Hampshire governor; Ralph Nader, consumer advocate and 2000 presidential candidate; Donna Shalala, former Secretary of Health and Human Services; Helen Thomas, a Hearst newspaper columnist; Khalil Gibran, poet-artist and author of *The Prophet*; Paul Anka, singer; William Peter Blatty, author of *The Exorcist* and other popular movie novels; Naomi Shihab Nye, a children's author of novels and poetry; John J. Zogby of Zogby International, a public opinion research firm; Dr. James J. Zogby, founder of the Arab-American Institute (AAI); Jack G. Shaheen, media analyst and author of *Reel Bad Arabs: How Hollywood Vilifies a People*; Christa McAuliffe, the teacher/astronaut who died aboard the space shuttle Challenger; Doug Flutie, National Football League quarterback and Heisman Trophy winner; and J.M. Haggar, clothing manufacturer (Haggar Slacks).

California has been home to many well-known Arab Americans, as well, including:

Darrell Issa, Congressman from Vista in San Diego County

Wadie Deddeh, former State Senator from Chula Vista (San Diego)

Candy Lightner, founder of Mothers Against Drunk Driving

Paul J. Orfalea, founder of Kinko's and the Orfalea Family Foundation

Casey Kasem and **Don Bustany**, creators of radio's American Top 40

Danny Thomas, the late actor and comedian

Marlo Thomas, daughter of Danny, and Emmy award winning actress

Jamie Farr, "Corporal Max Klinger" in TV series "M.A.S.H."

Kathy Najimy, actress

Paula Abdul, singer

Joe and **Gavin Maloof**, owners of the Sacramento Kings basketball team (See page 62.)

Sam Maloof, wood craftsman whose furniture is displayed in the White House and in leading museums nationwide. (See page 121.)

CHAPTER THIRTEEN

Inland Empire and Imperial Valley Arab Americans

THE INLAND EMPIRE has been the home of a number of Syrian-Lebanese families since at least 1939, according to the two Syrian-Lebanese directories. The lure appears unknown, unless it was the climate that reminded them of their homeland where citrus thrives. Emigrants from all parts of the world had been enticed to the area in the 1880s by the low fares offered by the Central Pacific Railroad. Perhaps Syrian-Lebanese peddlers, in later years, passed through the area themselves on this route or the Santa Fe Railroad that ran over Cajon Pass.

As early as 1939-40, Mike E. Hanna had a dry goods store in Ontario; in 1948-50 he owned a beer and wine store on Sultana Avenue and lived next door. In 1939-40 Saba Simon had a dry goods store on A Street, and Andrew and Alex Zlaket had a market on B Street. However, all three had moved to other locales by 1948-50. In 1948 Saba Simon had a ladieswear shop in Fontana on North 8th Street, and Alex Zlaket owned a market on Main Street in Riverside, where he still resides. (See page 133 for more about the Zlakets.)

The grandfather of the famous woodworker, Sam Maloof, sojourned in California at the turn of the 20th century, but returned to his home in Douma, Lebanon several years later. He left a daughter behind in Santa Barbara. Soon other Maloofs joined her.

Sam Maloof's parents, Nasif Slimen and Anise Nader Maloof, moved to Chino, where Sam was born their seventh child in 1916. The family eventually settled in Ontario where Nasif Maloof made a living as a merchant.

Sam Maloof is America's most widely admired contemporary furniture craftsman; his pieces are displayed in numerous museum collections and in the White House. Sam's son, Slimen Maloof, does woodworking himself, but spends more time working with the family foundation. The Sam and Alfreda Maloof Foundation for Arts and Crafts in Alta Loma awards scholarships to students of woodworking (Cain. *Arab-American Business* website; Sipchen *L.A. Times*).

Sam Maloof Craftsmanship

Photograph courtesy of Arab-American Business

Nassif N. Solomon also lived in Chino. A number of families lived or had vacation homes in Lake Arrowhead—even as early as 1939-40, including Joe Lazar, John Maloof, B. I. Malouf, Mrs. S. K. Mittry, and Norma Mittry Thomas. Construction of the dam for the reservoir had started in 1893 and continued through the early 1920s. It could be that one or more of the men from these families worked on that project.

By 1950 over 35 families lived in San Bernardino and many were operating small businesses. Carl Aide had a barbershop on Base Line Street. George Fallaha had a shoe shop on Third Street, and the Gabriel Bros. Department Store was located down the street. On Mt. Vernon Avenue, Haleen Joseph operated a variety store. Virgil Lopes ran a hardware and plumbing store on Highland Avenue; Elias Shaheen had a real estate office on Arrowhead Avenue; William Maloof had an auto dealership on E Street; Charles Gabriel had an ice company on E Street; and Shibli Damus owned a citrus shipping company on East Highland Avenue.

There were several grocers in San Bernardino, including Ernest Mitchell and David Mickel, both on Seventh Street. Dick Mickel sold beverages and Joe Richards sold meats.

Other residents included Edward Shaheen, Mrs. Joe P. Maloof, Mrs. A. Mickel, and Marshall J. Mickel. A few of these early families still live in San Bernardino today.

J. G. Maloof owned the Patsy Ann Department Store on South Sierra Avenue in Fontana, and George J. Nichols had a general merchandise store down the street. Charles Haddad Smith owned the Cottage Cafe on West Foothill Boulevard, and Nick Mickel ran a liquor store on Sierra Avenue. Saba Simon's ladieswear shop was already mentioned. Other residents of Fontana were Sam Coury and Naseem Thomas.

Shibli Damus lived in Colton. In addition to having his own citrus shipping company in San Bernardino, Shibli was the Fruit Commissioner.

Charles Bardawil owned a shoe store in Redlands. It probably was frequented by fellow Syrian-Lebanese— George A. Hackett and Jack Solomon.

In Riverside County, Dr. James Farrage operated a medical practice in the Corona Theater Building in Corona. He had graduated from the School of Medicine of the University of Southern California in 1936. He and his wife, Esther Synder, a nurse, had one son, James, who became an orthodontist. One of their three grandchildren is also a doctor, and the other two work in business and finance. (See page 126 for more details about the Farrage family.)

In the town of Riverside, the Andrews Bros. Ranch House was located on Iowa Avenue, and Victor Andrews was a citrus shipper. John Gabriel ran a menswear shop on Main Street and, as mentioned above, Alex Zlaket had a market on Main Street.

Four Syrian-Lebanese families lived in Beaumont, two as early as 1939-40, but it does not appear that they owned businesses. The residents included Mrs. Tom Abdelnour, Carl S. Munyer, Moses Soffa, and Mrs. Lester True.

In neighboring Banning, as early as 1939-40, Deeb Nasser owned a furniture store on Livingston Street, and Mrs. George Ellis owned a dry goods store on South San Gorgonio Avenue. Neither of these businesses were listed in the later 1948-50 Syrian-Lebanese directory. According to both directories, Albert Abdun-Nur owned the Desert Provision Co., and Mrs. J. J. Corey was a resident of Banning.

Mitchell L. Cory owned the Gents Furniture store on East Florida Avenue in Hemet. Farris Samra lived in Elsinore—today known as Lake Elsinore.

The dry climate of the Coachella Valley, in the central portion of Riverside County, had attracted at least 15 Syrian-Lebanese families by 1939 and another ten families by 1948. Today the valley is famous for having the greatest amount of date culture in the United States—an industry that began after the first dates were imported from Algeria in the 1880s. In the 1920s, date cultivation was encouraged by the U.S. Department of Agriculture in cooperation with private enterprise, but the early Syrian-Lebanese settlers did not appear to have any connection with this industry. Instead, they seemed to be small business owners catering to the everyday needs of the communities in which they lived.

Palm Springs was born in 1876 when Southern Pacific laid tracks through the Coachella Valley. It is possible that Syrian-Lebanese peddlers passed through the area in the late 19th/early 20th centuries. Both of the Syrian-Lebanese directories list George Ellis as the owner of the Ready-to-Wear Merchandise store in Palm Springs, and by 1948, S. P. Maloof was operating the Maloof Department Store on South Palm Canyon Drive. Today Gerry Maloof's Shop for Men remains in business at the same address.

Victor M. Sudaha had a cafe at South Palm Canyon Drive and Indio Road, possibly frequented by two other Syrian-Lebanese families—the George Beebes and W. B. Maloufs.

Indio began as a construction camp for the Southern Pacific builders in 1876. By at least 1939-40, Leo Ellis was running a cafe in Indio, and there was an Ellis Bros. men's store on Fargo Street. Mike Abdelnour, Mrs. George, Nick Abraham, and Charles, Robert, Saleem, and William Thomas were among the other Syrian-Lebanese residents.

Another branch of the Abdelnour family lived in Indio. Nick Abdelnour was born in Beirut, Lebanon in 1911, into an industrious merchant family that worked hard in order to be able to send their sons to school. But in the early 1930s Nick set out for America to escape the political upheaval and persecution of Christians plaguing his homeland.

Unfortunately, he was among those who were turned away at Ellis Island and sent to Latin America instead. But he was one of those who was determined to come to America. After living in Mexicali, Mexico, he arranged for admission to California through a combination of processes, including obtaining a work visa, marrying an American woman, and enlisting in the U.S. Army.

He settled first in Calexico and later in Indio, where he owned and operated a dry goods store. (The 1948-50 directory listed him as the owner of the Plaza Market on Requa Avenue.)

Nick and his wife raised a son and daughter, Nicholas and Lori, who both still live in the area. Growing up, Lori always marveled at her dad's fervor for America. "He certainly saw no need for his children to learn Arabic, for example. We were Americans! He was very proud of his service in World War II in the Army," she recalled. Later he was active in local politics, including serving as mayor of Coachella, and volunteering on the election campaigns of former U.S. Senator and Congressman John Tunney.

There were some other Abdelnours in Coachella. Mike G. Abdelnour was in real estate, and Mike T. Abdelnour and David Ellis owned Ellis and Abdelnour Market. Joe Hanna ran the Midnight Cafe on Highway 99, and George Thomas owned a men's furnishings store.

In the early years of the 20th century three different Syrian-Lebanese immigrant families settled along the California/Arizona border. In San Bernardino County, the town of Needles had been founded in 1883 when the Santa Fe Railroad arrived to take the place of the steamboats operating on the Colorado River. Perhaps it was the railroad by which E. M. Nichols arrived and eventually established his dry goods and shoe store on Front Street—at least by 1939-40.

Between 1924 and 1934, Blythe, in Riverside County, became the home of two Arab American families related through marriage. Three members of the Farrage Ayoub family had emigrated from Lebanon to the East Coast in 1902. Yaoute Ayoub and two of her teenage sons, George and Minem, arrived first. Farrage and the other four children were to join them soon, but in the meantime, Farrage and the youngest child died. One daughter was badly burned on her face as a child and feared the immigration officials

George, Minem & Yaoute Farrage

would not let her enter the United States because of the scars, so only James and Salimi arrived. At Ellis Island, through one of the common misunderstandings that took place in processing, the immigration officials listed the Ayoubs as having the last name of Farrage, so the family has carried that name ever since.

Yaoute had a brother who lived in Boston, so the mother and two boys moved to nearby Lawrence, Massachusetts, where George and Minem saved their earnings from employment in a shoe factory. The family eventually moved to Jerome, Arizona, where George and Minem established dry goods stores—each called The Boston Store. James eventually moved to Los Angeles to go to medical school. (See page 123.) Salimi and her husband, Charlie Karam, whom she met while in Massachusetts, opened a grocery store in Jerome.

Meanwhile, another family from Lebanon lived in Globe, Arizona—200 miles southeast of Jerome. George Halby and his wife operated a general store and were raising their four children. George's mother lived in Jerome where she had a grocery store and raised fighting chickens. In 1921 she played matchmaker and arranged the marriage of her 14 year-old granddaughter, Maggie Halby, and 31 year-old Minem.

In 1922, George married a "picture bride" from Lebanon. His sister who remained in Lebanon sent him a photograph of her best friend,

Maggie & Minem Farrage - 1921

Hasseba, and he immediately proposed.

In 1924, George and Minem, on the advice of Minem's doctor, moved their families to the dry climate town of Blythe, California. They established The Boston Store on North Main Street in 1925.

During the next ten years, the brothers invested in ranch, commercial, and residential property in Blythe. George and Hasseba increased the size of their family of three by six, and Minem and Maggie added five more children to their family of two.

George & Hasseba Farrage - 1922

Jim, George, Yaoute & Minem Farrage

In 1934 Minem died of cancer, leaving behind his wife, Maggie, now 27 years old, with seven children ages seven months to 12 years old. Within months her parents and three siblings moved to Blythe—moving into her house and helping her move into the living quarters located at the rear of The Boston Store. Five years later, George and his family moved to Los Angeles where he opened another store. (One of George and Hasseba's sons became a doctor, one daughter became a nurse, and the other children entered the business world.)

With George's departure from Blythe, the store was now completely Maggie's and continued as such until she closed it around 1950. She also helped her brothers, Joe and Mike Halby, open an ice cream parlor called the Rendezvous Malt Shop. After six years, the brothers turned the shop into a men's and women's clothing and jewelry store called Halby's. Maggie's son, Dick Farrage, began working in the store in 1942, eventually becoming a partner, and in 1960, buying his uncles out and renaming the store Dick Farrage Store for Men and Women. Dick retired in the 1980s and sold the store to his cousin, George Halby. Today George still owns and operates the renamed store, Halby's.

Yaoute, the courageous immigrant mother, died the day Pearl Harbor was attacked in 1941. During World War II, Gary Field, near Blythe, served as a flight-training site for the U.S. Army Air Corps. Maggie Farrage could always be found among the community volunteers helping out at the base. She was also very active in the St. Joan of Arc Catholic Church.

Maggie's son, Tom Farrage Jr., returned to Blythe after serving in the U.S. Navy during World War II, working in automobile, insurance, and real estate sales. He and his wife, Gladys Tooley, also Lebanese, raised their five children in Blythe—Christina, Lisa, Tom, John, and Meg. All of the children have since moved to other cities, although one granddaughter and her family remain in Blythe.

Tom and his brother, Dick, before he moved to Hemet, both served on the Blythe City Council, having between them over 20 years serving as council members and mayor. Since the late 1980s, Tom has played an active role in helping Blythe transition into serving as the site of two new state prisons. He also serves on the Blythe Chamber of Commerce and is active in the Catholic Church.

All of Minem and Maggie's other children moved to other parts of California and Arizona. Maggie's brother, Joe, had four children. Two of his sons, George and Joey, still live in Blythe with their families.

(Farrage family history and photographs courtesy of Meg and Tom Farrage.)

In 1901 water for irrigation and domestic purposes was diverted from the Colorado River through a canal that fed the Imperial Valley—initiating the valley's agriculture industry. In 1903 a branch line of the Southern Pacific railway reached Brawley. These two events, coupled with the availability of inexpensive land, drew early pioneers from other areas of the United States and from all over the world. By 1908 the Imperial Valley cities of Brawley, Calexico, El Centro, and Holtville had formed official governments.

According to the 1939-40 and 1948-50 Syrian-Lebanese directories, about 25 families were among the early settlers in the area. Some or all may have been immigrants who were rerouted to South America and finally realized their dream of living in the United States.

As early as 1939, 14 families lived in Brawley, but by 1948-50 six families had moved away—likely to more populated areas in Southern California. Gabe Abdelnour and George Abdelnour both operated grocery stores.

Saba, Mitchell, and Charles Ellis all lived at the same address. Charles and Nick Ellis owned a department store on Main Street; Charles Ellis also had a grocery store on North 10th Street. Abedel Gany Kutupe operated a dry goods store on East Main Street. There was an Eastern-rite Christian church in Brawley—the St. Elias Orthodox Church at 2nd and C Streets.

Gabe Abdelnour, the grocer already noted, and his wife, Mary, had come from Lebanon; they eventually owned and operated a number of other retail establishments and restaurants in Brawley. Their son, Charles Gabriel Abdelnour, currently is the City Clerk of San Diego. He also serves on the Executive Committee of the Arab American Institute in Washington, D.C. and the Executive Board of the Arab-American Leadership Council.

A dozen Syrian-Lebanese families lived in Calexico; many were operating businesses on Hefferman Street as early as 1939. A. Fares operated La Favorita Store at 13 Hefferman; Ernest Ellis and S. Ellis had a general merchandise store at 104 Hefferman; S. Thomas had a mercantile store at 107 Hefferman; Ed Jabway had a barber shop at 112 Hefferman; Joe Abdelnour & Sons had a general merchandise store at 117 Hefferman; and the Rashid Grocery was located at 127 Hefferman.

Other businesses were Raya Bros. on Second Street, Charles Thomas' Ladies Wear shop on Second Street, Rashid Bros. market and Pete Rashid's market, both on Third Street; N. J. Sleem's rug store on Third Street, and Farid Maloof's dry goods and grocery store on Fifth Street.

Other residents in Calexico included Richard and William Hashem, John Rashid, Kalil Smaha, and Najeeb Samaha.

The Lebanese Rashid family had sojourned in Argentina before arriving in Calexico. Descendants of this family and some of the other early Syrian-Lebanese families remain in Calexico today.

In El Centro, John Maloof sold groceries and S. Samaha had a dry goods store on Main Street. Descendants of both of these early families remain in El Centro today.

In Holtville, William Najeeb Samaha was operating a dry goods store as early as 1939-40. One of his sons, Ralph Samaha, was an active supporter of youth sports; when he passed away, an athletic field was named after him. Ralph's brother, Leo Samaha, is married to the current mayor pro tem of Holtville—Virginia Samaha.

Today the Coachella and Imperial valleys have very few Arab Americans living or working there. Although there are many Catholic churches in the two valleys, none appear to be Eastern-rite churches, and there are no Islamic centers or mosques. One Middle Eastern restaurant is located in Palm Springs—La Shank House Persian.

Music of the Arab World

- The music of the Arab world is a diverse mixture of musical characteristics and instruments played, due to the constant influx of peoples from other parts of the world. The music of this region has influenced the music of the West. Several Western world instruments derived from Arab world instruments.
- *Al-oud* has a half pear-shaped body, a 20-inch neck, and five or six double strings. It is played with an eagle's feather or a piece of plastic. The Arabic name means "the wood." The first Western descendant of al-oud (the oud) was the lute, and later the guitar.
- *Setar* is a long-necked lute with four strings and a small half pear-shaped sound box.
- *Tar* is a long-necked, fretted lute with five or six strings tuned in pairs. It has a double belly covered with a membrane of sheepskin.
- *Santour* is a flat zither-type instrument shaped like a trapezoid. Its 72 strings are played by striking them with two wands or hammers. It is the ancestor of the Western piano.

Adapted from "The Music of the Middle East and North Africa"
by Ayad Al-Qazzaz

CHAPTER FOURTEEN

Orange County Arab Americans

TODAY ORANGE COUNTY has one of the largest Arab American populations in the state, but this is a relatively recent development. By 1948-50, according to the Syrian-Lebanese directory, there were only about 55 such families in the county.

Farmland planted in orange groves, bean fields, strawberry beds, and flowers was the mainstay of Orange County's economy for many years, until the post-World War II boom, when cheap housing and the expanding defense and aerospace industries lured hundreds of thousands of people to the county. The opening of Disneyland in Anaheim in 1955 brought nationwide attention and resulted in tourism becoming the main driver of the economy. The county's diverse technological and business infrastructure continues to be a draw for immigrants from the Arab world.

Orange County is home to many Palestinians, and Anaheim is considered to be the only cohesive Arab American community in Southern California. There are numerous Eastern-rite Christian churches—Maronite, Melkite, Byzantine Catholic, and Antiochian and Greek Orthodox; a number of Islamic Society organizations, and several mosques or Islamic centers. There also are more than a dozen Middle Eastern restaurants in Orange County.

The 1948-50 directory lists two grocers, Charles Hazmalkolch and Murphy Zlaket, as operators of stores in Placentia. John Bashara, Simon Mansour, John Nahra, and Assaf Thomas resided in Placentia.

About a dozen Syrian-Lebanese families were living in Anaheim by 1948. A. and J. Anton and C. Mitchell had grocery

Anton's Food Market circa 1920
Courtesy Anaheim History Room,
Anaheim Public Library

stores on either end of Los Angeles Street, which today is Anaheim Boulevard.

Peter and Paul Arage ran Arage La Palma Grill and John Samon owned Samon Drive-In Restaurant on South Manchester Ave.

Other early Anaheim residents included Najib Attallah, Bahia Matouk Christensen, Mike George Ephrem, and John Matouk. When they were ill, they all probably went to see Dr. Aziz Araj in his office on South Los Angeles Street. Descendants of some of these families appear to remain in Anaheim today, but most Arab Americans in Anaheim are newer arrivals.

In 1948 Mr. Chaarani was a resident of Orange, and S. V. Mansur owned the Mansur Motor Company in town.

Approximately 15 Syrian-Lebanese families were living in Santa Ana by 1948-50, including Mrs. Abraham Ablan, Ben A. Craig, Haliem Ganamy, and E. C. Mitchell. Charles Kawaja operated a store on West Fourth Street, M. R. Gabriel owned an ice company, and R. S. Williams ran the Kelvinator Agency on North Broadway.

The Zlaket family, now four generations strong in California, settled in several locations in the 1920s. They made their start in America in southern Colorado when Kalil Zlaket emigrated from Zahle, Lebanon in the 1890s. He and his wife, Mary Basha from Nova Scotia, opened a market in Segundo, along the Colorado/New Mexico border. They raised their family of six boys and two daughters there.

When each son reached the age of 21, Kalil gave him $5,000 to start his own business, which several sons did in Colorado. But in the early 1920s most of the family migrated to Southern California. The two oldest sons, Murphy and Leo, opened a market in the area of Los Angeles known today as Watts.

In 1927, Leo and his wife, Mary Fikani, opened their own market in a store-front on Main Street in Garden Grove and welcomed the arrival of the first of three children. In 1937, they bought the property next door and built a new enlarged facility that also housed their living quarters above. Local newspaper articles featured them on the front pages, heralding the beauty and the latest in fixtures and design. Leo operated Zlaket's Food Market while Mary ran a dry goods store in the building next door where they had started out.

In 1950 Leo and Mary turned the family business over to their oldest son, George; the youngest son, Leo II,

Leo, David & Virginia Zlaket

became a partner in 1962, when he turned 21. Today, Leo, his wife, Virginia Roman (whose father emigrated from Hardeen, Lebanon to Pittsburgh, Pennsylvania), and their son, David, continue the Zlaket legacy of hard work, perseverance, and maintaining family ties and the strength of their relationships.

Over the years, in order to compete with newer markets, the store has changed —operating as a gourmet meat market in the 1950s and moving into the catering, deli, and specialty foods market business in the mid-'80s, which remains the focus today.

(Zlaket family history and photograph courtesy of Virginia Zlaket.)

The 1948-50 Syrian-Lebanese directory listed Mansour Anton, of the Anton's Food Market pictured on page 133, and S. Steven Basha as residents of Costa Mesa; Marshall Nickels operated a market on Newport Boulevard. In Laguna Beach, Victor Andrews, Mrs. J. J. Corey, Nasef Ellis, and S.K. Saba were residents, and John M. Peters operated a store for men on Coast Boulevard. Ed Chade operated a market on El Camino Real in San Juan Capistrano.

Traditional Arab Dress

- Most Arab Americans do not wear traditional clothing, but those who do, do so as a religious practice, not a cultural practice. It is rooted in Islamic teachings about *hijab*, or modesty. The purpose of *hijab* is not to belittle women, but to protect them from unwanted sexual attention. At home with family and female friends, casual dress is acceptable.
- Covering is not universally observed by Muslim women and varies by region and class. The governments of various Arab countries have, at times, banned or required veiling, a black cloth (*bushiya*), or a mask (*burqa*). (The most conservative form of the burqa leaves only a mesh screen to see through.)
- The practice of *hijab* can include wearing long clothing (*caftan, abaya, abayah, jilbab,* or *chador*) and a scarf (*hejab, hijab,* or *chador*). Beneath a robe, a woman may be wearing a traditional dress, casual clothes, or a business suit, but she never allows anyone to see the dress while she is outside. Black may be worn in mourning for a few days to many years.
- In Arab American families, a mother or daughter may cover her head while the other does not. Ironically, the scarves that Muslim women have worn for centuries as protection against sexual harassment and aggression are now not being worn in America for fear that they incite anti-Arab and anti-Muslim aggression. Most Muslim women in the United States do not wear veils that cover the face.
- Some Arab men wear a white, long loose gown (*dishdasha, djellaba, bisht, thob,* or *thobe*) and a turban. The style in which a turban is wound and the knot used to tie it vary from region to region and follow ancient traditions.
- Some Arab men wear a checked garment on their heads (*kafiyyeh, gatra,* or *ghutra*), but it is not religious. The headdress is held in place by a twisted black rope (*iqal, agul,* or *agal*) and shows identity and pride in one's culture. A skullcap is usually worn under the checked garment.
- A man's headgear is often a sign of his social status. A lower class man might wear a small, close-fitting cap with geometric patterns on it, while a wealthier man would wear a maroon-colored fez. No Muslim would ever wear a hat with a brim, because this would prevent him from touching the ground with his forehead when saying his prayers.

CHAPTER FIFTEEN

San Diego County Arab Americans

TODAY SAN DIEGO is the second largest city in the state and the sixth largest in the nation, so it is understandable that it would have one of the largest concentrations of Arab Americans. These are recent occurrences.

Despite the fact that a rail line connected San Diego to the east through Barstow as early as the mid-1880s and a land boom followed, industry and trade growth was sporadic and never was strong enough to support newcomers to the area until the outbreak of World War I in 1917. In that year, San Diego was chosen as the site for the War Department's Army Division in the Southwest. Over time that designation led to the subsequent interest in the area from other branches of the military. Soon San Diego acquired a growing defense and aerospace industry that provided jobs for new arrivals, including highly skilled engineers from the Arab world.

Before this later larger immigration, however, a few Syrian-Lebanese made their way to this coastal community that had a climate similar to what they had left behind in Syria and Lebanon.[53]

The 1939-40 Syrian-Lebanese directory lists 35 families residing and working in the City of San Diego and the 1948-50 issue lists over 70 families. Residents included Fred, Eva,

[53]The Panama-California International Exposition was held in Balboa Park in 1915 and 1916. Although no historian has ever conjectured that this exposition was a catalyst for emigration from the Arab world to San Diego as earlier expositions in other American cities had been, it certainly is likely. There was a wide variety of fine art and industrial exhibits from Egypt, and a concessionaire, who managed a "Holy Land" exhibit, sold jewelry, rugs, laces, religious carvings, and crosses. Word likely spread about the Mediterranean climate in San Diego.

and Sadie Ashook; Al Boushala, Louis Naassery, and several branches of the Barrack family—Frank, George, Louis, and Mrs. Mary Barrack.

Alec L. Cory was an attorney on Dove Street; Michael Addas was a doctor; and George Addas was a shoemaker. Henry Saleebey sold insurance on Saratoga Avenue, and Mike Ellis operated a general merchandise store on Ninth Street.

Louis Castellani and Walter Sawaya both had service stations—on 25th Street and National Boulevard, respectively. Ted Saleebey had a nursery on Tivoli Street.

A large number of families were involved in the grocery business. The Fare families had markets throughout town, including Margaret Fare's on National Avenue and Nasim Fare's on El Cajon Boulevard. Hikel Bros. grocery was on National Avenue, and Charles Hikel operated a beverage store on Logan Avenue. Carl Mulki had a grocery store at 30th and K streets, Fred Nader one on Sampson Street, and Gabe Saliba one on 18th Street. Sawaya Bros. market was on Logan Avenue, and Afefe Sawaya had a grocery store on Imperial Avenue. There were at least seven other adult members of the Sawaya family in San Diego at this time; the family was listed in the San Diego City Directory as early as 1920.

Descendants of most of the families named above remain in San Diego today and have since been joined by other Arab Americans from a variety of locales in the Arab world. There are at least two Eastern-rite Christian churches in San Diego—St. Anthony Antiochian Orthodox Christian Church and St. George Antiochian Orthodox Church, as well as the Islamic Society of San Diego, the Islamic Center of San Diego, and two mosques, which most likely have Arab Americans as part of their congregation.

There also are numerous Middle Eastern restaurants in San Diego County, including Hajji Baba Restaurant, El

Embarcadero, Fairouz Restaurant & Gallery, Alladin Mediterranean Cafe & Gourmet Market, Azul La Jolla, and Marrakesh.

Nadim Farrar emigrated from Beirut, Lebanon to the East Coast in 1923. He began his engineering career in Pennsylvania, arriving in California in 1943. Before his death 40 years later, he went on to design many of San Diego County's highway bridges and assist in the design of foundations for the University of California, San Diego Medical Center and the San Diego Jack Murphy Stadium ("Obituary, Nadim Farrar").

There are families related to the Shaieb family of Aleppo, Syria, in Alameda, Long Beach, and San Diego. The Shaiebs of San Diego began arriving in 1947 after first spending 30 to 35 years in Detroit, Michigan.

In 1911, when the Melkite Catholics in Syria were being persecuted by the Muslims, 24-year-old Nagib Shaieb set out from Aleppo for Ellis Island and New York City. Within a year, he moved to Detroit to take an automobile assembly job with the Ford Motor Company.

In 1913 Nagib asked his father in Aleppo to find him a wife. Soon his father, a neighbor, and his neighbor's 15-year-old daughter, Afify, arrived in Detroit. Unaware of the pre-arranged marriage plans, Afify thought she was going on a vacation to America. Instead, she was meeting the man she would spend the next 49 years with and bear seven children with, one of whom died as a toddler.

After Nagib left Ford Motors in 1922, he opened his own grocery

Shaieb Grocery in Detroit

Shaieb Family in Detroit

store in Detroit. All of the family worked in the store at one time or another and it was the training ground for George, Edward, Julie, and William, who would eventually have their own grocery stores in San Diego.

Nagib retired from the grocery store business in 1946. When he and Afify were vacationing and visiting friends in San Diego the next year, they fell in love with the Mediterranean feel of the community and decided to spend the rest of their lives there, which they did.

Nagib soon missed having the opportunity to meet and greet people, however, so he opened a small store in the back of his house on El Cajon Boulevard in La Mesa. He sold Middle Eastern food to those fortunate enough to hear about his store by word of mouth.

In the ensuing years, the six grown children and their families—16 children between them—moved to San Diego, as well. Those who continued in the grocery store business were quite successful, including

Shaieb Family in California

Edward, who opened one of the first multi-purpose grocery stores in La Mesa—Eddie's Supermarket.

Joseph had a dental practice in San Diego for 27 years before retiring and moving to Santa Barbara, where he volunteers at

140

the information desk of the main hospital. William eventually left the grocery store business and became an independent plumber and real estate investor. Virginia also invested in real estate and Edward became a real estate broker after selling his store. Edward also was a Meals on Wheels volunteer for 18 years, delivering food to senior citizens, before he passed away in 1995. Julie was a Meals on Wheels volunteer, as well.

The grandchildren pursued different careers, including 7-Eleven franchise ownership, real estate investment, fire fighting, medicine, physical therapy, and radio station management. They all remain in Southern California, with the exception of one, who is an orthopedic surgeon in Florida, and another, Albert, who died in 1999. Albert was a fireman in El Cajon for many years before he retired.

One granddaughter, Dona Shaieb, describes her grandfather's life as follows: "His life in California was a sort of paradise for a man who fled religious persecution, leaving behind his homeland to find freedom and a place to achieve his dreams. He died happily having accomplished all that he had hoped he would."

(Shaieb family history and photographs courtesy of Dona Shaieb.)

Outlying San Diego communities had a few entries in both the 1939-40 and 1948-50 Syrian-Lebanese directories. Mrs. Mary George Jones lived in Oceanside and may have shopped at Mrs. Peter Nader's ladies wear shop on North Hill Street and George Owen's ladies and children's wear shop on Hill Street. The Daher George family lived in Carlsbad; Cory Alex owned a dry goods store in town.

Three generations of Shelhoups have owned and operated businesses in downtown Vista since the early 20th century. In 1928 Mike Shelhoup and his son, Abraham, both natives of Douma, Lebanon, moved to Vista after a sojourn in Brawley.

They purchased a grocery store and butcher shop, later adding dry goods to their line of merchandise. They continued to work together until 1936 when Abraham bought his father's interest. Two years later Abraham sold the market and established a variety store. In 1941 he opened the Shelhoup Department Store at a different location, selling only name-brand merchandise.

Until his death in 1981, Abraham continued his contributions to the city by building the Avo Theatre, which the city recently renovated and reopened as the popular Avo Playhouse; donating 286 trees and two fountains to beautify the city, and playing an active role in All Saints Episcopal Church, Rotary, the Shriners, and other community activities.

Abraham and his wife, Hayat, also a native of Douma, Lebanon, produced a son, Kamal, who assumed ownership of his father's store until he closed it in 1996. A year later Kamal opened Antiques On Main Street—located in the same building, which today is part of a Historic Walking Tour of Downtown Vista (Doyle 346).

Kamal has continued his father's practice of community involvement by serving on various boards of directors, including Rotary, the Vista Chamber of Commerce, the Boys and Girls Club, YMCA, and the Vista Town Center Association. He also was the chairman of the Downtown Master Plan Committee between 1983 and 1985 (Shelhoup interview).

Kamal has a Ph.D. in Public Administration and Public Law. He also is an accomplished pilot and flight instructor.

In Encinitas, Shickrey Cory operated a general merchandise store on First Street where the Lafayette Baida family probably shopped.

South of San Diego, in National City, Mrs. Eva Hobica owned the Lad & Lassie Shop on East 8th Street, and the Ramos' owned Gents Furniture on National Avenue. Abe and Leon N. Cory were residents of National City. Dr. Ayoub, George L. Cary, and Simon Tamer lived in Chula Vista.

In San Ysidro, Mike Bujazan was a theater manager and Mike Ellis was operating a general merchandise store in 1929. George Bujazan, Sidney Elias, and Toofik Hourani lived there, as well.

Finally, a branch of the Cory family was the first Arab family to live in El Cajon in 1948. Tuffey Cory was a manager at Safeway. The Cory family was Lebanese, but today El Cajon has an especially large population of Kurds from northern Iraq.[54]

Another branch of the Cory family, Abraham and Melia Cory, emigrated from Lebanon in the early 1900s, started their family in Colorado in 1906, and later moved to Oceanside where they operated a shoe store. (Melia lived to be 102 years old.)

Sometime in the 1950s, their married daughters, Julia Cory Potter and Eva Cory Hobica, opened the Jul-Eve Store in the South Bay Shopping Center in National City. (Eva had earlier owned Lad and Lassie Children's Store in National City.) The two sisters produced children's fashion shows for the shopping center, the community, and charitable organizations ("Obituary, Eva Cory Hobica" *San Diego Union-Tribune*).

[54]Today more than 25,000 Iraqis live in San Diego County—the largest such community in the United States behind Detroit (McDonald, et al. *San Diego Union-Tribune*). Arabs are represented in this population, but the majority is Chaldean and Kurdish. Most fled Iraq in 1975 to escape persecution under Saddam Hussein's regime.

Epilogue

THE FOREGOING information about some of the early and more recent arrivals of immigrant families from the Arab world is intended to provide a sense about this freedom-loving, hard-working, entrepreneurial, family and community-oriented ethnic group in California. The characteristics and family stories repeat themselves throughout the state and the country.

Communicating with these families revealed a wide array of responses. Some knew their family history well; others worked very hard to learn it with my prodding. I hope that all of these families are pleased with the result of our collaboration together.

Some knew nothing about their family history and did not know where to begin. A few, whose families arrived in America in the first wave of immigration under the ethnic label of Syrian or Lebanese, still do not consider themselves to be Arab Americans. There is much they can learn in this book to help them understand their heritage.

Arab Americans may appreciate the presentation of an objective look at their roots in the Golden State, but I also wrote for the larger audience of non-Arab Americans. It is my hope that this book will promote understanding to replace ignorance and bigotry. If California and other parts of the country that have diverse populations are to thrive in the 21st century, people need to be knowledgeable about the various ethnic groups that make our country the unique place that it is today.

This book is a start and it is appropriate that the focus is on Arab Americans, as they appear to be the most misunderstood ethnic group in America. The Federal Bureau of Investigation's annual survey of hate crimes released in November 2002 reported that Arabs and others who appeared to be Muslim were threatened, beaten, and generally discriminated against more in 2001 than at any other time in the past. The prejudices against this ethnic group remain high, fueled by 9/11, but anchored by negative and inaccurate pre-conceptions about Muslims and Arabs—even Christian Arabs.[55]

Look for *California: An International Community—Understanding Our Diversity,* to be released in 2004; it will provide interesting information about California's many other ethnic groups. Space in a book about all of the major groups will not allow the detail and individual stories contained in this book, but there will be a summary about why and when each group arrived in California and why some settled in particular locations.

Janice Marschner
janicemar@comcast.net

---

[55] A California Department of Justice report released in July 2003 found that the number of anti-Arab/anti-Middle East hate crimes in California dropped significantly in 2002 (Korber *Sacramento Bee*).

Bibliography

Books

Abraham, Sameer Y. and Nabeel Abraham, eds. *Arabs in the New World: Studies on Arab-American Communities*. Detroit: Wayne State University Press, 1983.

Abu-Laban, Baha and Michael W. Suleiman, eds. *Arab Americans: Continuity and Change*. Belmont, MA: Association of Arab-American University Graduates, 1989.

___ and Faith T. Zeady, eds. *Arabs in America: Myths and Realities*. Wilmette, IL: Medina University Press International, 1975.

Allen, James P. and Eugene Turner. *The Ethnic Quilt, Population Diversity in Southern California*. Northridge, CA: The Center for Geographical Studies, California State University, 1997.

Al-Qazzaz, Ayad. *Transnational Links Between the Arab Community in the U.S. and the Arab World*. Sacramento: California State University, Sacramento, 1979.

Ameri, Anan and Dawn Ramey, eds. *Arab American Encyclopedia*. Detroit: Arab Community Center for Economic and Social Services, 2000.

Archbold, Norma Parrish. *The Mountains of Israel – The Bible & the West Bank*. Israel and USA: Phoebe's Song, 2002.

Ashabranner, Brent. *An Ancient Heritage: The Arab-American Minority*. New York: HarperCollins Publishers, 1991.

Aswad, Barbara C., ed. *Arabic Speaking Communities in American Cities*. Staten Island: Center for Migration Studies of New York, 1974.

Brooks, Jack. *Front Row Center: A Guide to Northern California Theatres*. San Francisco: 101 Productions, 1981.

Brown, Roslind Varghese. *Tunisia, Cultures of the World*. New York: Marshall Cavendish, 1998.

Brown, Wesley and Amy Ling, eds. *Visions of America: Personal Narratives from the Promised Land*. New York: Persea Books, 1993.

Cooper, Robert. *Bahrain*. New York: Marshall Cavendish, 2001.

Doyle, Harrison and Ruth. *The History of Vista*. Vista, CA: Hillside Press, 1983.

Eck, Diana L. "American Muslims: Cousins and Strangers." Condensed version of a chapter from *A New Religious America: How a "Christian Country" Has Become the World's Most Religiously Diverse Nation.* New York: HarperCollins, 2001.

Flink, Andrew. *A Century of Cinema in Sacramento, 1900-2000.* Rancho Cordova, CA: The Author, 1999.

Fox, Mary Virginia. *Bahrain, Enchantment of the World.* Chicago: Childrens Press, 1995.

Friedlander, Jonathan, Ron Kelley, and Sheila Pinkel, eds. *Sojourners and Settlers: the Yemeni Immigrant Experience.* Salt Lake City: University of Utah Press; Los Angeles: G. E. Von Grunebaum Center for Near Eastern Studies, University of California at Los Angeles, 1988.

Galens, Judy, Anna J. Sheets, and Robyn V. Young, eds. *Gale Encyclopedia of Multicultural America.* Detroit: Gale Research, 1995.

Gerner, Deborah J., ed. *Understanding the Contemporary Middle East.* Boulder, CO and London: Lynne Rienner Publishers, 2000.

Goodwin, William. *Saudi Arabia.* San Diego: Lucent Books, 2001.

Haddad, Yvonne Y. and Jane I. Smith, eds. *Muslim Communities in North America.* Albany, NY: University of New York Press, 1994.

Haiek, Joseph R., ed.-pub. *The American Arabic Speaking Community 1975 Almanac.* Los Angeles: The News Circle, 1975.

____. *The American Arabic Speaking Community 1984 Almanac.* Los Angeles: The News Circle, 1984.

Hall, Loretta. *Arab American Voices.* Detroit: U.X.L., The Gale Group, 2000.

____ and Bridgett K. Hall. *Arab Americans Biography.* Vol. 1 & 2. Detroit: U.X.L., The Gale Group, 1999.

Harik, Elsa Marston. *The Lebanese in America.* Minneapolis: Lerner Publication Company, 1987.

Harmon, Daniel E. *Sudan – 1880 to the Present: Crossroads of a Continent in Conflict.* Philadelphia: Chelsea House Publishers, 2000.

Hitti, Philip K. *The Syrians in America.* New York: George H. Doran Company, 1924.

Hooglund, Eric J., ed. *Crossing the Waters: Arabic-Speaking Immigrants to the United States before 1940.* Washington, D.C.: Smithsonian

Institution Press, 1987.

Johns, Stephanie Bernardo. *The Ethnic Almanac.* Garden City, NY: Doubleday, 1981.

Johnson, Julia. *United Arab Emirates.* Philadelphia: Chelsea House Publishers, 2000.

Kagda, Falaq. *Algeria, Cultures of the World.* New York, London, Sydney: Marshall Cavendish, 1997.

Kallen, Stuart A. *Egypt, Modern Nations of the World.* San Diego: Lucent Books, 1999.

Kayal, Philip M. *An Arab-American Bibliographic Guide, Bibliography Series No. 4, October 1985.* Belmont, MA: The Association of Arab-American University Graduates, Inc., 1985.

Kern County Centennial Observance Committee. *Kern County Centennial Almanac.* Bakersfield: Kern County Centennial Observance Committee, 1966.

Lamb, David. *The Arabs – Journeys Beyond the Mirage.* New York: Vintage Books, 2002.

Mehdi, Beverlee Turner, ed. *The Arabs in America, 1492-1977.* Dobbs Ferry, NY: Oceana Publications, Inc., 1978.

Mulloy, Martin. *Saudi Arabia.* Philadelphia: Chelsea House Publishers, 1999.

Naff, Alixa. *Becoming American: the Early Arab Immigrant Experience.* Carbondale, IL: Southern Illinois University Press, 1985.

____. *The Arab Americans–The Immigrant Experience.* Philadelphia: Chelsea House Publishers, 2002.

Orfalea, Gregory. *Before the Flames: A Quest for the History of Arab-Americans.* Austin: University of Texas Press, 1988.

O'Shea, Maria. *Kuwait–Cultures of the World.* New York, London, Sydney: Marshall Cavendish, 1999.

Reedley Historical Society and Fresno Pacific College. *Reedley - A Study of Ethnic Heritage: A Study of Selected Ethnic Groups Playing a Major Role in the Historical Development of Reedley.* Reedley, CA: Reedley Historical Society, 1998.

Sady, Rev. Elias, ed. *Fifth Issue (1939-1940) of the Syrian Directory of the State of California.* Los Angeles: Saint George's Church, 1940.

____. *Sixth Issue (1948-50) of the Directory of California American*

Arabic-speaking people from Syria, Lebanon, Palestine and the Levant. Los Angeles: Saint George's Church, 1950.

Sanders, Renfield. *Libya.* Philadelphia: Chelsea House Publishers, 2000.

Sifri, Randra. "San Francisco, California - Arab Culture in the Bay Area." Eds. James Zogby, Pat Aufderheide, and Anne S. Mooney. *Taking Root, Bearing Fruit: The Arab-American Experience.* Washington, D.C.: American-Arab Anti-Discrimination Committee, 1984.

Slide, Anthony. *The New Historical Dictionary of the American Film Industry.* Lanham, MD: Scarecrow Press, Inc., 2001.

Suleiman, Michael W., ed. *Arabs in America - Building a New Future.* Philadelphia: Temple University Press, 1999.

Temple, Bob. *The Arab Americans - We Came to America.* Philadelphia: Mason Crest Publishers, 2003.

Thernstrom, Stephan, Ann Orlov, and Oscar Handlin, eds. *Harvard Encyclopedia of American Ethnic Groups.* Cambridge, MA: Belknap Press, 1980.

Waldinger, Roger and Mehdi Bozorgmehr, eds. *Ethnic Los Angeles.* New York: Russell Sage Foundation, 1996.

Wilkins, Frances. *Morocco, Major World Nations.* Philadelphia: Chelsea House Publishers, 2000.

Wills, Karen. *Jordan–Modern Nations of the World Series.* San Diego: Lucent Books, Inc., 2001.

Younis, Adele L. Ed. Philip M. Kayal. *The Coming of the Arabic-Speaking People to the United States.* Staten Island: Center for Migration Studies, 1995.

Zogby, James, Pat Aufderheide, and Anne S. Mooney. *Taking Root, Bearing Fruit: The Arab-American Experience.* Washington, D.C.: American-Arab Anti-Discrimination Committee, 1984.

Periodicals

"Builder Edward G. Romley Dies" obituary. *Contra Costa Times* 23 Sept. 1965:?

Conlin, Bill. "Solons Stay Here After Stock Sale." *Sacramento Union* 24 Dec. 1954: 1.

Curley, Douglas K. "Giving Back to the Community - Sacas of Filco

Reflect on Philanthropy." *Comstock's* Dec. 1997: 69-70.

"Edward Shaieb, 74; was grocery store owner, broker, volunteer."*San Diego Union-Tribune.* 29 Jan. 1995.

Glackin, William. "Local Man Hopes For Fortune From His Wartime Invention." *Sacramento Bee* 19 Aug. 1948: ?

"George Sady, Poultry Dealer, Dies at 58" obituary. *Sacramento Union* 18 July 1963:?

"James E. Nasser" obituary. *Variety* - Garland Publishing, Inc. 335 (5-11 July 1989):106-109.

"Kaisser Azar" obituary. *Santa Barbara News-Press* 30 May 1972: ?

Korber, Dorothy. "Anti-Arab hate crimes drop sharply, state says." *Sacramento Bee* 16 July 2003: A3.

"Koury services" obituary. *Santa Barbara News-Press* 5 June 5 1977: ?

Kulczycki, Andrzej and Arun Peter Lobo. "Deepening the Melting Pot: Arab-Americans at the Turn of the Century." *The Middle East Journal* 55, Iss. 3 (Summer 2001): 459.

"Lee Naify, 61, Manager For Theater, Dies." *Sacramento Bee* 17 Sept. 1959:?

Levin, Steve. "The Theatres of the San Francisco Bay Area." *Marquee, The Journal of the Theatre Historical Society of America* 23, No. 3 (Third Quarter 1991): 8-26.

Luby, Earle B. "Ganim Says Gulch Land Is Good -- If You'll Work Hard." *Redding Record-Searchlight* ? Mar. 1947: 10.

"The Maloofs Have Built a Business Empire by Helping People Have Fun - Family is Involved in Basketball, Gambling, Liquor — and Politics." *Arab-American Business* 1, Issue 10 (Aug. 2001): 16-17, 22.

Mattson, Eric. "Public defender: Nice guy, tough job - Judge, DA praise new appointment." *Sacramento Bee* 13 Aug. 1989: B1-2.

McDonald, Jeff, Michael Stetz and Angela Lau. "A jubilant day for many Iraqis here." *San Diego Union-Tribune* 10 Apr. 2003: ?

"Michael Selby" obituary. *Santa Rosa Press Democrat* 1 Nov. 1996: B2.

"Milton Maloof" obituary. *Santa Rosa Press Democrat* 24 Oct. 1999: B2.

"Mrs. Koury Busy Grocer on Store's 46th Anniversary." *Santa Barbara News-Press* 21 Sept. 1965: ?

"Obituary, Eva Cory Hobica." *San Diego Union-Tribune* 29 Dec.

1999: ?

"Obituary, Nadim Farrar." *San Diego Union-Tribune* 22 Nov. 1983: ?

"Old Phone Book Brings Reunion After 21 Years." *Santa Rosa Press Democrat* 11 May 1921: ?

"Raymond Syufy" obituary. *Variety* - Garland Publishing, Inc. 358 (10-16 April 1995): 58.

"Richard J. Nasser" obituary. *Variety* - Garland Publishing, Inc. 333 (23 Nov. 1988): 110-111.

Shaheen, Jack G. "The media's image of Arabs." *Newsweek* 29 Feb. 1988: 10.

"Shalhoob Rites" obituary. *Santa Barbara News-Press* 26 Apr. 1968: ?

Sipchen, Bob. "A Man of the Woods - The Sunday Profile." (Sam Maloof) *Los Angeles Times* 24 July 1994: E2.

Slater, Pam. "Salamy soon to retire as county public defender." *Sacramento Bee* 10 Apr. 1993: B1-2.

Weissberg, Al. "Cascade Theatre - The Beginning." Shasta Historical Society - *Covered Wagon* 1998: 90-96.

____. "The Cascade Theatre Story - Part II." Shasta Historical Society - *Covered Wagon* 1999: 46-49.

Miscellaneous and Unpublished Materials

1990 Census: "Profiles of Selected Arab Ancestry Groups." C3.223/ 12: 1990 CPS-1-2.

Abdelnour, Lori. E-mail interview Apr. 2003.

Abdun-Nur, John. Completed questionnaire to author. Mar. 2003.

Al-Qazzaz, Ayad, Rosalie Cuneo Amer, and Dr. Viviane Doche. *The Arab Community in Sacramento: A Historical and Social Portrait.* Sacramento Ethnic Communities Survey completed for the Sacramento History Center in 1984.

Al-Qazzaz, Ayad. "The Music of the Middle East and North Africa." *SAAA Program for The Ninth Annual Middle East Culture & Food Festival.* Sacramento Association of Arab Americans. 8 Sept. 2001.

____. In person and e-mail interviews Feb., June 2003.

Amer, Dr. Metwalli. "A Brief History of 16 Years In the Life of

SALAM (1987-2002)." Sacramento Area League of Associated Muslims website. http://www.salamcenter.org/.

___. E-mail interviews April, May 2003.

Amer, Prof. Rosalie Cuneo. E-mail interviews July 2003.

Anderson, Jen. "The Old Lady is 75 - Theatre Anniversary." *Castro Star*. May 1997. http://www.webcastro.com/casstar.htm #THEAT.

Ayoob, Nicholas. Telephone interview Jan., May 2003.

Bracken, Phil. Letter to the author. 21 April 2003; telephone interview April, May 2003.

Brown, Vernon A. "Re: Info. on Arab Americans." E-mail to author. 6, 7 April 2003.

Cain, Sandi. "Arab-Americans Have a Major Presence in the U.S. Tech Capital." *Arab-American Business*. http://www.arabamericanbusiness.com/March2002/coverstory.htm.

___. "Personality Profile: 'I Hope my Furniture has a Soul.'" *Arab-American Business*. http://www.arabamericanbusiness.com/December%202002/index_december2002.htm.

"California Death Records." RootsWeb.com. http://vitals.rootsweb.com/ca/death/search.cgi.

Colivas, Jerry. Letter to the author. June 2003; e-mail to author July 2003.

Educational Guide to the Arab and Muslim World. San Francisco: Arab Cultural Center, 2001.

Farrage, Tom and Meg. Telephone and e-mail interviews. Apr., May, June 2003.

Freeman, Dennis. "Re: Requesting info. on two early Weed residents." E-mail to author. 14 May 2003.

Ganim, Joe. Telephone interview. June 2003.

Gerawan, Dan. Testimony before Subcommittee on Commercial and Administrative Law, Committee on the Judiciary, U.S. House of Representatives Taxpayers Defense Act. 29 July 1999. http://www.house.gov/judiciary/gera0729.htm.

Getz, Monica. "Vista's birthday bash recalls 40 years of cityhood." *North County Times* 26 Jan. 2003. http://www.nctimes.net/news/2003/20030126/65929.html.

Ghazi, Jalal. "'Arab Afghan' Primer—Who are the Ones Who Got

Away?"*Pacific News Service*, 29 Mar. 2002. http://news.pacificnews.org.

Haddad, Elias W. "Chuck". Completed questionnaire to author. Mar. 2003.

"Hamas - Harakat al-Muqawamah al-Islamiyya." The International Policy Institute for Counter-Terrorism http://www.ict.org.il/inter_ter/orgdet.cfm?orgid=13.

Homsy, Adele, George M. (Bud) Homsy, and Barbara Homsy Lithin. Letter to the author and e-mail interviews. Mar., June, July 2003.

Homsy, George. "This is Your Life George Edward Homsy Sr." 1988:1-21.

Humboldt County Historical Society. "Re: Davis Schemoon's general merchandise store in Eureka." E-mail to author. 3 Apr. 2003.

"Kais Menoufy - Founder, President and CEO." Delegata website. http://www.delegata.com/about/kaism.asp.

Kelley, Tim. "Cliff's." *Castro Star*. June 1997. http://www.webcastro.com/casstar.htm#CLIFF.

Kuttab, Daoud. "The Third Intifada." 28 Sept. 2002. *Arabic Media Internet Network*. http://www.mediamonitors.net/kuttab54.html.

Lawson, Scott, Plumas County Museum. Telephone interview March 2003.

Maloof Sports and Entertainment. http://arcoarena.com/default.asp?lnopt=4&pnopt=0

Malouf, Gail. E-mail interviews. Mar., July 2003.

Martinez Historical Society. Letter to the author. 12 Apr. 2003.

Menoufy, Kais. E-mail interview. June, July 2003.

Morgan, Ronald S. "Re: Arab Americans in Ft. Bidwell & Alturas." E-mail to author. 9 April 2003.

Naify, Jane. In person interview and e-mail letters July, Aug. 2003.

Naify, Jim. Telephone interview June 2003.

"Naseeb Michael Saliba Business Leader Lebanese 1997 Recipient." Ellis Island Medal of Honors website http://www.neco.org/awards/recipients/saliba.html.

Nasser, Theodore D. Letter to the author. 2 July 2003.

"Patterns of Global Terrorism, 2002." U.S. Department of State Apr. 2003. http://www.state.gov/s/ct/rls/pgtrpt/2002/html.

Producer's Dairy. "Our History." http://www.producersdairy.com.

Rashid, Alma. Completed questionnaire to author. Mar. 2003.

Romley, James and Audrey. Telephone interview; letter to author April 2003.

Sacramento Association of Arab Americans. *SAAA Program for The Ninth Annual Middle East Culture & Food Festival.* 8 Sept. 2001.

San Diego Historical Society. Letter to the author. 17 April 2003.

Santa Barbara Historical Society. Letter to the author.. 20 June 2003.

Shaieb, Dona. E-mail interviews Apr., May 2003.

Shelhoup, Kamel. Telephone interview; completed questionnaire to author. May, June 2003.

Shibley, William H. Completed questionnaire to author. Mar. 2003.

Suleiman, Michael W. "History, Demography and Identity." Woodrow Wilson International Center for Scholars. (2001) http://wwics.si.edu/topics/pubs/ACF21B.pdf.

Thomas Aquinas College Quarterly Newsletter. Spring 1999. http://www.thomasaquinas.edu/news/newsletter/1999/spring/zeiter.htm

University of Southern California, School of Medicine of USC website.http://www.usc.edu/schools/medicine/alumni_resource/class_agent/.

Vista Historical Society. Letter to the author. 26 Mar. 2003.

Western Federation American-Syrian-Lebanon Clubs convention program, held at Hollywood Roosevelt Hotel, July 2-5, 1948.

Wingfield, Marvin and Bushra Karaman. "Arab Stereotypes and American Educators." American-Arab Anti-Discrimination Committee. (March 1995) http://www.adc.org/index.php?id=283.

Winkler, Harleigh. "Re: [CA Calaveras] Fahily - shoemaker in San Andreas in 1948." E-mail to author. 27 May 2003.

Zahn, Willard F., M.D. Letters to author. Mar., June, July 2003.

Zeidner, Robert F. "From Babylon to Babylon: Immigration from the Middle East. *People of Utah.*" http://historytogo.utah.gov/mideast.html.

Zlaket, Virginia. E-mail interviews Mar., Apr. 2003.

"Zoot Suit Riots - People & Events: George E. Shibley (1910-1989)". PBS website http://www.pbs.org/wgbh/amex/zoot/eng_peopleevents/p_shibley.html.

INDEX

About the Author

JANICE MARSCHNER is a California history writer and independent publisher from Sacramento, California. A native Californian, her interest in the history of her state crystallized in 1995 with a visit to a California State Park in the gold country. That visit inspired her to write her award-winning *California 1850 - A Snapshot in Time*, published in time to commemorate California's sesquicentennial in 2000.

Janice is a graduate of the University of California, Davis with a degree in International Relations and the California State University, Sacramento with a Masters in Public Policy and Administration. Until she retired in June 2000, she spent eleven years working in California state government.

Her future books in progress are *California: An International Community—Understanding Our Diversity* and *California's Early Hot Springs Resorts*.

Visit the Coleman Ranch Press website at
www.CRPRESS.com

Coming: Fall 2004

California: An International Community
Understanding Our Diversity

By: Janice Marschner

- Overview of immigration to California—why and when the state's various ethnic groups arrived and why some located in certain areas.
- Summary of the social and economic circumstances that caused America to become the most diverse nation in the world.
- Description of the culture and recent history of the homelands of foreign-born Americans.

Intended Readership

- Adults and high school/college students who have neither the time nor inclination to read volumes of sociological/historical texts, but who seek to understand our international community.
- Those working on their genealogy will love the book. Discover what your parents or grandparents never told you about the circumstances of your ancestors' arrival in America.
- A welcome addition to the reference section of all public and school/university libraries.

ISBN: 0-9677069-5-5
History/Regional/Multicultural
$25 - $30
6" x 9", Hard Cover
250-300 pages

Coleman Ranch Press
www.CRPRESS.com
colemanranch@comcast.net
1.877.7OLDCAL
Fax: 1.888.532.4190